50 Literacy Strategies

Step by Step

Fourth Edition

GAIL E. TOMPKINS

California State University, Fresno, Emerita

PEARSON

Boston   Columbus   Indianapolis   New York   San Francisco   Upper Saddle River   Amsterdam
Cape Town   Dubai   London   Madrid   Milan   Munich   Paris   Montreal   Toronto
Delhi   Mexico City   São Paulo   Sydney   Hong Kong   Seoul   Singapore   Taipei   Tokyo

Vice President, Editor-in-Chief: Aurora Martínez Ramos
Executive Development Editor: Hope Madden
Editorial Assistant: Michelle Hochberg
Executive Marketing Manager: Krista Clark
Production Editor: Janet Domingo
Editorial Production Service: Cenveo Publisher Services
Manufacturing Buyer: Megan Cochran
Electronic Composition: Cenveo Publisher Services
Interior Design: Cenveo Publisher Services
Cover Designer: Diane Lorenzo

Credits and acknowledgments borrowed from other sources and reproduced, with permission, in this textbook appear on the appropriate page within text.

Library of Congress Cataloging-in-Publication Data

Tompkins, Gail E.
  50 literacy strategies : step by step / Gail E. Tompkins. -- 4th ed.
  p. cm.
  Includes bibliographical references and index.
  ISBN 0-13-294491-X
  1. Language arts (Elementary)--United States. 2. Language arts (Middle school)--United States. I. Title. II. Title:
  Fifty literacy strategies.
  LB1576.T653 2013
  372.6--dc23

                                                                            2012008749

10 9 8 7 6 5 4 3 2 1

www.pearsonhighered.com

ISBN 10: 0-13-294491-X
ISBN 13: 978-0-13-294491-5

Contents

Preface

· ·

The fourth edition of *50 Literacy Strategies: Step by Step* is a conveniently organized resource for all elementary and middle school teachers, providing research-based and classroom-tested strategies that develop literacy abilities. This thoroughly revised new edition—loaded with information on adapting instruction, implementing standards, and integrating technology—offers a rich resource for all prospective and practicing literacy teachers in elementary and middle schools.

Everything you need to implement each instructional strategy—appropriate grade level, adaptations for English learners, information on when and why to use the strategy, and a step-by-step description of the procedure—is included in a consistent, easy-to-understand format.

The instructional focus and consistent format make these strategies easy to use in the classroom. Each activity begins with a grid that identifies the most appropriate use and answers the following questions at a glance:

- Does the strategy best develop oral language, phonemic awareness/phonics, fluency, vocabulary, comprehension, writing, spelling, and/or content areas?
- For what grade level(s) does the strategy work best?

Following this opening matrix, each step-by-step strategy is organized around the why, how, and when of using the procedure.

Each instructional strategy begins with a brief discussion that covers why the particular activity is effective. Then a clear, step-by-step description of implementation walks you through the procedure. Student samples further illustrate the classroom application, and a section on when to use the activity helps you situate each instructional strategy into your teaching day.

Within these sections you'll also find the research driving each strategy and additional tools to make the strategy as effective as possible: specific information about adapting instruction for English learners, ideas for differentiating instruction to meet the needs of all students, strategy-specific information on integrating technology, connections to the Common Core State Standards for English Language Arts, and Booklists to highlight classroom applications.

NEW TO THIS EDITION

A strengthened focus on adapting instruction for all students, as well as new guidance on integrating standards and technology, makes this revision a powerful choice for today's classrooms.

- **Three new strategies** discuss Possible Sentences, Process Drama, and RAFT.
- **Differentiating Instruction** sections in certain chapters describe ways to adapt the instructional strategy to meet the needs of all students.

- **Go Digital** features in certain chapters suggest ways to integrate digital technology resources such as podcasts and Inspiration software into the instructional strategy.
- **Common Core State Standards for English Language Arts** features pinpoint the ways individual strategies connect to this important set of standards.
- **Booklist** features identify mentor texts teachers can use when teaching a particular instructional strategy.

ADDITIONAL KEY FEATURES

- Scaffolding English Learners sections provide direction on adapting the instructional strategies to meet diverse student needs.
- Strategies are arranged alphabetically and numbered for easy reference.
- Inside the front cover is a matrix categorizing strategies by the appropriate Common Core State Standards for English Language Arts.

COURSESMART EBOOK AND OTHER EBOOK OPTIONS AVAILABLE

CourseSmart is an exciting new choice for purchasing this book. As an alternative to purchasing the printed book, you may purchase an electronic version of the same content via CourseSmart for reading on PC, Mac, as well as Android devices, iPad, iPhone, and iPod Touch with CourseSmart Apps. With a CourseSmart eBook, readers can search the text, make notes online, and bookmark important passages for later review. For more information or to purchase access to the CourseSmart eBook, visit http://www.coursesmart.com. Also look for availability of this book on a number of other eBook devices and platforms.

1   "All About . . ." Books

Instructional Focus		Grade Levels
☐ Oral Language	☐ Comprehension	☑ PreK–Grade 2
☐ Phonemic Awareness/Phonics	☑ Writing	☐ Grades 3–5
☐ Fluency	☐ Spelling	☐ Grades 6–8
☐ Vocabulary	☑ Content Areas	☑ English Learners

Young children write "All About . . ." books on familiar topics (Tompkins, 2012). They put together a booklet with four or five pages, write a sentence or two on each page, and add illustrations to elaborate the information presented in the text. Students read the book to the teacher, who helps them elaborate ideas and correct mechanical errors before they share from the author's chair (see p. 10). As they gain experience writing books with one or two sentences per page, students can expand and elaborate the information they share on each page, gradually increasing the length to a paragraph.

WHY USE THIS INSTRUCTIONAL STRATEGY

This is one of the first types of books that many young children or other beginning writers make. The organization is simple, with one piece of information written and illustrated on each page. It's a successful writing experience for both beginning writers and their teachers because it's completed quickly—usually in a day or two—and easily.

Scaffolding English Learners

Making an "All About . . ." book is an excellent activity for English learners of any age who are novice writers. The book's structure is easy to learn: They write a piece of information about a topic using a sentence or two on each page and add an illustration. Those students who are very artistic embellish their books with impressive, detailed illustrations that extend the information presented in the text. English learners can work individually, with a partner, or in a small group to write an "All About . . ." book to share what they've learned about a topic that interests them.

COMMON CORE STATE STANDARDS FOR ENGLISH LANGUAGE ARTS: "ALL ABOUT . . ." BOOKS

This instructional strategy supports these Common Core State Standards for Reading: Informational Text and Writing:

- Students read grade-appropriate informational texts.
- Students share the results of research through writing.
- Students write informative/explanatory texts.

Students make important connections between reading and writing as they craft "All About . . ." books.

HOW TO USE THIS INSTRUCTIONAL STRATEGY

This writing activity fits easily into prekindergarten through second grade classrooms because most students can write "All About . . ." books independently once they're familiar with the procedure. Teachers follow these steps:

1 **Choose a topic for the book.** Students choose a topic that's familiar or interesting to them, or teachers suggest a broad topic related to a thematic unit the class is studying.

2 **Gather and organize ideas for writing.** Students brainstorm possible ideas for what they'll write on each page, or they draw pictures for each page.

3 **Write the book.** Students write a sentence or two on each page to accompany pictures they've drawn.

4 **Read the book with the teacher.** Students conference with the teacher, reread their books, and make revising and editing changes as necessary. Students often add more words to what they've written, correct spelling errors, and insert necessary punctuation marks. Sometimes teachers or students word process final copies after the conference, or they "publish" their books without recopying them.

5 **Share the completed book with the class.** Students sit in the author's chair to read their completed books to classmates. Then classmates clap, offer congratulatory comments, and ask questions.

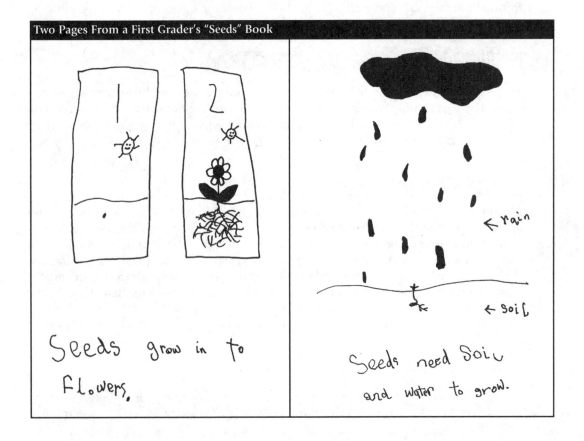

Two Pages From a First Grader's "Seeds" Book

Seeds grow in to Flowers.

Seeds need Soil and water to grow.

← rain

← soil

WHEN TO USE THIS INSTRUCTIONAL STRATEGY

Students often make "All About . . ." books as part of thematic units and during writing workshop. During thematic units, students write these books to share what they're learning. The figure on the previous page shows two pages from a first grader's "Seeds" book. This child wrote about information he learned during the unit, and he spelled most of the words correctly by locating them on a word wall (see p. 156) posted in the classroom. The few remaining errors were corrected during a conference with the teacher.

During writing workshop, students choose their own topics for these books, writing about their families, pets, vacations, hobbies, and other experiences. For example, a first grader wrote this book about "My Precious Cat" during writing workshop:

Page 1: My cat is named Meow because she meows and meows all the time.

Page 2: I feed Meow Cat Chow in her dish every morning.

Page 3: Meow got lost once for 6 days but then she came home. She was all dirty but she was safe.

Page 4: Meow is mostly all black but she has white on her toes. Her fur is very silky.

Page 5: Meow sleeps on my bed and she licks me with her scratchy tongue.

This student wrote about a familiar topic, and on each page of her book she focused on a different piece of information about her cat.

Differentiating Instruction

"All About . . ." books are very adaptable. Teachers individualize instruction to meet students' needs using these adaptations:

- Students create wordless books using drawings with captions and diagrams with labels.
- Students work with partners or in small groups to complete their pages.
- Students draw a picture on each page and dictate an explanatory sentence that the teacher writes underneath using the Language Experience Approach (see p. 64).
- Students add a visual component by writing labels for their drawings to highlight important information.
- Students write longer texts to accompany their illustrations, often a paragraph or two in length.

Through these adaptations, students create books successfully and apply what they're learning about written language.

REFERENCES

Tompkins, G. E. (2012). *Teaching writing: Balancing process and product* (6th ed.). Boston: Pearson.

2 Alphabet Books

Instructional Focus		Grade Levels
☐ Oral Language	☐ Comprehension	☐ PreK–Grade 2
☐ Phonemic Awareness/Phonics	☑ Writing	☑ Grades 3–5
☐ Fluency	☐ Spelling	☑ Grades 6–8
☑ Vocabulary	☑ Content Areas	☑ English Learners

Y ou may be familiar with the alphabet books that young children make with a scrapbook-like collection of words and pictures representing each letter, but older students create more sophisticated alphabet books using technical vocabulary words to share what they're learning during a thematic unit (Evers, Lang, & Smith, 2009). They construct 26-page alphabet books with one page featuring each letter, much like the alphabet trade books published for older children, including *D Is for Dragon Dance* (Compestine, 2006), *America: A Patriotic Primer* (Cheney, 2002), *Jazz ABZ* (Marsalis & Schaap, 2005), and *The Accidental Zucchini: An Unexpected Alphabet* (Grover, 1997). Turn to the Booklist on the next page for additional books. The words chosen for less common letters, such as *e, k, q, u,* and *y,* are especially interesting to check. Students choose vocabulary words beginning with each letter of the alphabet, write explanations describing how the word relates to the topic, and add illustrations to extend the text. Then the pages are compiled and bound into a book, and these books are added to the classroom library for students to read.

WHY USE THIS INSTRUCTIONAL STRATEGY

Michael Graves (2006) explains that students need multiple, meaningful experiences with words to expand their vocabularies, and when students create an alphabet book, that's just what they're doing. They talk about words they're choosing and read and write about them. They make connections between the words and the big ideas they're learning as they create an authentic project—a book that they'll read and that students in next year's class will read.

Scaffolding English Learners

Expanding English learners' vocabulary is crucial because their word knowledge significantly affects their achievement. As they participate in alphabet book projects, English learners review and refine their understanding of content-area words and make connections between the words and the big ideas they're learning. In addition, they often reread these class books after they've been published and use them as a resource when they're writing other books.

COMMON CORE STATE STANDARDS FOR ENGLISH LANGUAGE ARTS: *ALPHABET BOOKS*

This instructional strategy supports these Common Core State Standards for Writing and Language:

• Students learn grade-appropriate vocabulary related to novels and thematic units.
• Students write informative texts to explain the meaning of key vocabulary.

Students deepen their understanding of academic vocabulary as they make alphabet books.

BOOKLIST

Alphabet Books

Cheney, L. (2003). *A is for Abigail: An almanac of amazing American women.* New York: Simon & Schuster. M.

Dugan, J. (2005). *ABC NYC: A book about seeing New York City.* New York: Abrams. M.

McLeod, B. (2008). *SuperHero ABC.* New York: HarperCollins. M

Osornio, C. L. (2010). *The Declaration of Independence from A to Z.* Gretna, LA: Pelican. M

Segal, R. (2007). *ABC in Washington, DC.* New York: Murray Hill Books. MU

Shoulders, D., & Shoulders, M. (2010). *G is for gladiator: An ancient Rome alphabet.* Ann Arbor, MI: Sleeping Bear Press. MU

Sobel, J. (2009). *Shiver me letters: A pirate ABC.* New York: Sandpiper. P

Spradlin, M. P. (2010). *Baseball from A to Z.* New York: HarperCollins. MU

Strother, R. (2011). *B is for blue planet: An earth science alphabet.* Ann Arbor, MI: Sleeping Bear Press. M

Wilbur, H. L. (2008). *Z is for Zeus: A Greek mythology alphabet.* Ann Arbor, MI: Sleeping Bear Press. MU

P = primary grades (preK–2); M = middle grades (3–5); U = upper grades (6–8)

HOW TO USE THIS INSTRUCTIONAL STRATEGY

Students usually make alphabet books collaboratively as a class. Small groups or individual students can make alphabet books, but with 26 pages to complete, it's an arduous task. Teachers follow this procedure:

1 **Examine alphabet books.** Students examine the format and design of sophisticated alphabet trade books published for children that present words beginning with each letter and include information about the words and illustrations.

2 **Prepare an alphabet chart.** Teachers write the letters of the alphabet in a column on a long sheet of butcher paper, leaving space for students to write several words beginning with that letter on the chart. Students brainstorm words for the alphabet chart, and they write the words on the paper next to the appropriate letter. Students often consult the word wall and reference books in the classroom as they try to think of words for each letter.

3 **Choose a letter.** Students consider which word they can explain best through writing and art and then sign up for that word's letter on a sheet the teacher has posted in the classroom.

4 **Design the page format.** Students consider where the letter, the illustration, and the text will be placed on the page and decide on the pattern for the text. Younger students might write a single sentence of text (___ is for ___ because ___), but older students add more information about their topics and write a paragraph or two.

5 **Use the writing process to create the pages.** Students use the writing process to draft, revise, and edit their pages. Then they make the final copies of the pages and add illustrations. Sometimes they handwrite the final copies, or they use a computer to print out professional-looking pages.

6 **Compile the pages.** Students and the teacher put the pages in alphabetical order, design a cover, and bind the book.

WHEN TO USE THIS INSTRUCTIONAL STRATEGY

Alphabet books are often used as projects at the end of thematic units, such as the oceans, the desert, World War II, or California missions, as well as after reading novels and biographies (Fordham, Wellman, & Sandman, 2002). The "U" page from a fourth grade class's

The "U" Page From a Fourth Grade Class Alphabet Book

alphabet book on the California missions is shown here. Sometimes a little ingenuity is required to think of a word for less common letters; the fourth graders' choice of the word *unbearable* for *u* shows both their vocabulary knowledge and their comprehension of the big ideas presented during the unit.

REFERENCES

Cheney, L. (2002). *America: A patriotic primer*. New York: Simon & Schuster.

Compestine, Y. C. (2006). *D is for dragon dance*. New York: Holiday House.

Evers, A. J., Lang, L. F., & Smith, S. V. (2009). An ABC literacy journey: Anchoring in texts, bridging language, and creating stories. *The Reading Teacher, 62*, 461–470.

Fordham, N. W., Wellman, D., & Sandman, A. (2002). Taming the text: Engaging and supporting students in social studies readings. *The Social Studies, 93*(4), 149–158.

Graves, M. F. (2006). *The vocabulary book: Learning and instruction*. New York: Teachers College Press.

Grover, M. (1997). *The accidental zucchini: An unexpected alphabet*. San Diego: Voyager.

Marsalis, W., & Schaap, P. (2005). *Jazz ABZ*. Cambridge, MA: Candlewick Press.

3   Anticipation Guides

Instructional Focus		Grade Levels
☑ Oral Language	☑ Comprehension	☐ PreK–Grade 2
☐ Phonemic Awareness/Phonics	☐ Writing	☐ Grades 3–5
☐ Fluency	☐ Spelling	☑ Grades 6–8
☐ Vocabulary	☑ Content Areas	☐ English Learners

Students complete anticipation guides (Head & Readence, 1992) before reading content-area textbooks and nonfiction books to activate background knowledge. Teachers prepare a list of statements about the topic that students discuss before reading; some of the statements are true, and others are incorrect or based on common misconceptions. Students discuss each statement and decide whether they agree with it. Then after reading the selection, students again discuss the statements and decide again whether they agree with them (Readence, Bean, & Baldwin, 2004). Usually students change some of their opinions, and they realize that they've refined their understanding of the subject through the activity.

An anticipation guide about a chapter on immigration in a social studies textbook, for example, might include these statements:

> There are more people immigrating to the United States today than ever before.
> The government sets a quota for the number of people from each country allowed to enter the United States each year.
> Most people immigrate because they want better jobs.
> Aliens are people who are in the United States illegally.
> Refugees are people who are forced to flee from their homeland because of war or other disasters.
> Many immigrants have difficulty adjusting to life in America.

You probably agree with some of these statements and disagree with others, and perhaps you're unsure about a couple of them. Having these questions in mind when you begin reading sets a purpose for reading and helps direct your attention to the big ideas. As you read, you might find that your initial assessment of one or two statements wasn't accurate, and when you repeat the assessment after reading, you'll make some changes.

COMMON CORE STATE STANDARDS FOR ENGLISH LANGUAGE ARTS: *ANTICIPATION GUIDES*
This instructional strategy supports the Common Core State Standards for Reading: Informational Text:

- Students read and comprehend grade-appropriate nonfiction texts, including textbooks.
- Students draw on information from print and digital sources.
- Students demonstrate the ability to locate information in texts quickly.

Students deepen their understanding of nonfiction texts as they complete anticipation guides.

WHY USE THIS INSTRUCTIONAL STRATEGY

The purpose of this activity is to stimulate students' interest in the topic and to activate background knowledge, and after students discuss anticipation guide statements, they're better prepared to comprehend the reading assignment. The follow-up discussion after reading also clarifies the big ideas and brings closure to the reading activity.

HOW TO USE THIS INSTRUCTIONAL STRATEGY

Students work together as a class or in small groups to discuss the statements and decide which ones are accurate before and again after reading. Teachers follow these steps as they use this procedure:

1 **Identify several major concepts related to the reading assignment.** Teachers keep in mind students' knowledge about the topic and any misconceptions they might have about it.

2 **Develop a list of statements.** Teachers prepare four to six statements that are general enough to stimulate discussion and clarify misconceptions. They can be written on a chart or on a sheet of paper that's then duplicated so that students can have individual copies. The guide has space for students to mark whether they agree with each statement before reading and again after reading.

3 **Discuss the anticipation guide.** Teachers introduce the anticipation guide and have students respond to the statements. Working in small groups, in pairs, or individually, students think about the statements and decide whether they agree or disagree with each one. Then, as a class, they discuss their responses to each statement and defend their positions.

4 **Read the text.** Students read the text and compare their responses to what's stated in the reading material.

5 **Discuss each statement again.** Students talk about the statements again, citing information in the text that supports or refutes each one. Or, students can again respond to each of the statements and compare their answers before and after reading. When students use the anticipation guide, teachers have them fold back their first set of responses on the left side of the paper and then respond to each item again on the right side.

WHEN TO USE THIS INSTRUCTIONAL STRATEGY

Although anticipation guides are more commonly used to activate background knowledge before reading nonfiction books and content-area textbooks, they can also be used with novels that explore complex issues, including homelessness, democratic societies, crime, and immigration. One eighth grade class, for example, studied about gangs in preparation for reading S. E. Hinton's *The Outsiders* (2006), and they completed the anticipation guide shown on the next page before and after reading the novel. The statements about gangs in the anticipation guide probed important points and led to lively discussion and thoughtful responses.

| Anticipation Guide on Gangs | | | | | |
| Before Reading | | Gangs | After Reading | | |
Agree	Disagree		Agree	Disagree
		1. Gangs are bad.		
		2. Gangs are exciting.		
		3. It is safe to be a gang member.		
		4. Gangs make a difference in a gang member's life.		
		5. Gangs fill a need.		
		6. Once you join a gang, it is very difficult to get out.		

REFERENCES

Head, M. H., & Readence, J. E. (1992). Anticipation guides: Using prediction to promote learning from text. In E. K. Dishner, T. W. Bean, J. E. Readence, & D. W. Moore (Eds.), *Reading in the content areas* (3rd ed.; pp. 227–233). Dubuque, IA: Kendall/Hunt.

Hinton, S. E. (2006). *The outsiders*. New York: Penguin.

Readence, J. E., Bean, T. W., & Baldwin, R. S. (2004). *Content area literacy: An integrated approach* (8th ed.). Dubuque, IA: Kendall/Hunt.

4 Author's Chair

Instructional Focus		Grade Levels
☐ Oral Language	☐ Comprehension	☑ PreK–Grade 2
☐ Phonemic Awareness/Phonics	☑ Writing	☑ Grades 3–5
☐ Fluency	☐ Spelling	☑ Grades 6–8
☐ Vocabulary	☐ Content Areas	☐ English Learners

A special chair in the classroom is designated as the author's chair (Graves & Hansen, 1983). This chair might be a rocking chair, a lawn chair with a padded seat, a wooden stool, or a director's chair, and it should be labeled with a sign identifying it as the "Author's Chair" (Karelitz, 1993). Students sit in this chair to share their writing with classmates, and this is the only time anyone sits there. They share their writing at different stages in the writing process: When they share rough drafts, students want feedback from classmates about how they can revise their writing, and when they share their published writing, students are celebrating the completion of a writing project. Teachers at all grade levels use author's chairs, but these special chairs are most important in primary classrooms where students are developing a concept of authorship (Graves, 1994).

WHY USE THIS INSTRUCTIONAL STRATEGY

Donald Graves and Jane Hansen (1983) have documented students' growing awareness of authors and of themselves as authors. They found that first, students learn that authors write books. After listening to many books read to them and after reading books themselves, they develop the concept that authors are the people who write books. Next, students realize that because they write books, they're authors, too. Sharing the books they've written with classmates from the author's chair helps students view themselves as authors. Third, students learn that they have options when they write, and this awareness grows after they have experimented with various writing purposes, forms, and audiences. After sharing their books with classmates and listening to classmates' comments, they realize that if they were to write one of their books now, they wouldn't write it the same way.

COMMON CORE STATE STANDARDS FOR ENGLISH LANGUAGE ARTS: *AUTHOR'S CHAIR*

This instructional strategy supports these Common Core State Standards for Reading: Foundational Skills and Writing:

- Students write for varied audiences.
- Students publish their writing.
- Students read accurately and with expression to support comprehension.

Students develop as readers and writers as they share their writing from the author's chair.

HOW TO USE THIS INSTRUCTIONAL STRATEGY

Students use the author's chair as part of writing workshop, and usually the entire class is involved in sharing their writing and responding to their classmates' writing. Teachers follow these steps as they use this procedure:

1 **Choose a special chair.** Teachers often purchase child-size chairs or rocking chairs at yard sales for their author's chair. They add a sign identifying the special chair as the "Author's Chair." Chairs can be painted and the sign stenciled on. Other teachers purchase director's chairs or lawn chairs to use.

2 **Explain how the author's chair will be used.** Student-authors will sit in the chair to share their writing with classmates during writing workshop or other writing activities.

3 **Sit in the author's chair.** One student sits in the author's chair, and classmates sit on the floor or in chairs in front of the author's chair.

4 **Share writing.** The student reads a piece of writing aloud and shows the accompanying illustrations.

5 **Invite listeners to comment.** Students raise their hands to offer compliments, ask questions, and make other comments about the book.

6 **Call on classmates.** The student sitting in the author's chair calls on two or three classmates to offer comments, and then the student chooses a classmate to sit in the author's chair.

GO DIGITAL

Vodcasts
Students create video podcasts of classmates sharing their writing from the author's chair. Student filmmakers need a digital video camera, such as a Flip camera, set on a tripod and an external microphone. After filming, they upload the video onto a computer, use editing software, and add background music. Then vodcasts are placed on the classroom website for students and parents to view.

WHEN TO USE THIS INSTRUCTIONAL STRATEGY

The author's chair is a social routine that can be used during any phase of the writing process to ask classmates for feedback and support about their writing or to showcase their completed writing projects. Labbo (2004) suggests having students create a high-tech author's chair using a computer and a large-screen monitor: The writing is displayed so classmates can read it themselves or read along with the student who is reading it aloud. Then they can make comments and suggestions. One of the benefits of "author's computer chair" is that students can share their computer knowledge and expertise.

REFERENCES

Graves, D. H. (1994). *A fresh look at writing*. Portsmouth, NH: Heinemann.

Graves, D. H., & Hansen, J. (1983). The author's chair. *Language Arts, 60,* 176–183.

Karelitz, E. B. (1993). *The author's chair and beyond*. Portsmouth, NH: Heinemann.

Labbo, L. D. (2004). Author's computer chair. *The Reading Teacher, 57,* 688–691.

5 Book Boxes

Instructional Focus		Grade Levels
☐ Oral Language	☑ Comprehension	☑ PreK–Grade 2
☐ Phonemic Awareness/Phonics	☐ Writing	☑ Grades 3–5
☐ Fluency	☐ Spelling	☑ Grades 6–8
☐ Vocabulary	☑ Content Areas	☑ English Learners

Book boxes are collections of objects and pictures related to a particular story or informational book. After reading a book, students decorate the outside of a box or other container and collect three to five objects and pictures related to the book. Then they put the items they've collected in the box along with a copy of the book or other reading material. The items should be significant to understanding the book. For example, a book box for *The Giver* (Lowry, 2006) might include an apple, a toy bicycle, a card with the number 19, a toy sled, and a hypodermic syringe from a child's toy doctor kit.

Students can also make book boxes after reading nonfiction books and biographies. For instance, after reading *Bread, Bread, Bread* (Morris, 1989), a second grade class brought in sliced white bread, bagels, tortillas, pita bread, pretzels, French baguettes, cinnamon rolls, a pizza, and other kinds of bread. Children took photos of each kind for their book box and marked the bread's country of origin on a world map. Then they ate the bread and wrote about their favorite kinds. The teacher collected the writings, bound them into a book, and added the book to the book box, too. After reading Jean Fritz's *And Then What Happened, Paul Revere?* (1996), a fifth grader covered a box with aluminum foil to make it look like silver and added a portrait of Paul Revere he had drawn, a strip of paper with the patriot's lifeline, a fork to symbolize the silver Paul Revere made, a tea bag for the Boston Tea Party, and postcards of the Boston area that the student's aunt sent to him.

Teachers also make book boxes to use with books they share with students. For example, a book box for *The Mitten* (Brett, 2009) might contain yarn and knitting needles, a pair of white gloves, and small stuffed animals or pictures of animals (including a mole, a snowshoe rabbit, a hedgehog, an owl, a badger, a fox, a brown bear, and a mouse). Teacher-made book boxes are especially useful to share with young children, English learners, and struggling readers.

COMMON CORE STATE STANDARDS FOR ENGLISH LANGUAGE ARTS: *BOOK BOXES*

This instructional strategy supports these Common Core State Standards for Reading: Literature and Reading: Informational Text:

- Students comprehend grade-appropriate fiction and nonfiction books.
- Students determine the structure of stories and main ideas and details in nonfiction texts.
- Students interpret visual information.

Students demonstrate their comprehension as they make and share book boxes.

WHY USE THIS INSTRUCTIONAL STRATEGY

Book boxes are visual representations that enhance students' comprehension of books they're reading. Students refine their understanding as they create a book box and select important objects and pictures to include, and when teachers share book boxes that they've made before students read, they build students' background knowledge and introduce vocabulary to prepare them to read a book.

Scaffolding English Learners

Teachers often use book boxes with English learners because they can teach vocabulary and build background knowledge with the objects in the boxes. As students handle and talk about the objects, they become familiar with the words and how to use them in sentences; this preparation makes the reading experience more successful.

HOW TO USE THIS INSTRUCTIONAL STRATEGY

Sometimes students make individual book boxes, and at other times, they work together in small groups to create a book box. Teachers follow this procedure as they teach students to make book boxes:

1 **Read the book.** As students read or reread a book, they make a list of important objects mentioned in it that they might want to include in a book box.

2 **Choose a container.** Students choose a box, basket, plastic tub, empty coffee can, bag, or other container to hold the objects, and they decorate it with the name of the book or the topic and related pictures and words.

3 **Fill the book box.** Students place three to five (or more) objects and pictures in the box along with a copy of the book. They might also include an inventory sheet with all the items listed and an explanation of why each item was selected.

4 **Share the completed box.** Students share their book boxes with classmates, showing each item in the box and explaining why it was included.

GO DIGITAL

Slide Shows
After students collect items and pictures for their book boxes, they can use a digital camera to take pictures of the items and then create a slide show with Smilebox (http://www.smilebox.com) or another application. They can choose special features, including sparkles and swirls as well as background music and other special effects, to make their slide shows very professional.

WHEN TO USE THIS INSTRUCTIONAL STRATEGY

Students often make book boxes as a project during a literature focus unit or literature circle, but there are many other ways that this instructional strategy can be used. Here are five suggestions:

- **Author Boxes.** When students are studying favorite authors, they can make a box with collections of the author's books, biographical information about the author, a letter the student wrote to the author, and, with luck, a response from the author.

- **Autobiography Boxes.** Students can collect objects and pictures that represent each year in their lives and place them in a box that they've decorated.

- **Poetry Boxes.** Students can collect objects and pictures that represent a favorite poem and place them in a decorated box along with a copy of the poem.

- **Bio Boxes.** After reading a biography, students can collect objects and pictures related to the person and place them in a box or other container.
- **Theme Boxes.** As part of a thematic unit, students can collect objects, pictures, and books related to the theme and place them in a decorated box.

As students create each type of box, they identify important ideas and find ways to express the ideas visually.

REFERENCES

Brett, J. (2009). *The mitten*. New York: Putnam.

Fritz, J. (1996). *And then what happened, Paul Revere?* New York: Putnam.

Lowry, L. (2006). *The giver*. New York: Delacorte.

Morris, A. (1989). *Bread, bread, bread*. New York: Scholastic.

6 Book Talks

Instructional Focus		Grade Levels
☑ Oral Language	☑ Comprehension	☑ PreK–Grade 2
☐ Phonemic Awareness/Phonics	☐ Writing	☑ Grades 3–5
☐ Fluency	☐ Spelling	☑ Grades 6–8
☐ Vocabulary	☑ Content Areas	☐ English Learners

Book talks are brief teasers that teachers give to introduce students to new books and to interest them in reading the books. To hook students' interest, the teacher shows the book, summarizes it without giving away the ending, and reads a short excerpt aloud. Then teachers pass the book off to an interested reader or place it in the classroom library for students to read.

Students use the same steps when they give a book talk, and they often give book talks when they share the books they've read during reading workshop. Here's a transcript of a third grader's book talk about Paula Danziger's *Amber Brown Is Not a Crayon* (2006a):

◉ This is my book: <u>Amber Brown Is Not a Crayon</u>. It's about these two kids—Amber Brown, who is a girl, and Justin Daniels, who is a boy. See? Here's their picture. They are in third grade, too, and their teacher—his name is Mr. Cohen—pretends to take them on airplane trips to the places they study. They move their chairs so that it's like they're on an airplane and Amber and Justin always put their chairs side by side. I'm going to read you the very beginning of the book. [She reads the first three pages aloud.] This story is really funny, and when you're reading, you think the author is telling you the story instead of you reading it. And there are more stories about Amber Brown. This is the one I'm reading now—<u>You Can't Eat Your Chicken Pox, Amber Brown</u> [2006b].

There are several reasons why this student and others in her class are so successful in giving book talks: The teacher has modeled the procedure, and students are reading books that they've chosen—books they really like. In addition, these students are experienced in talking with their classmates about books.

Robb (2000) calls book talks *the reader's chair*, which focuses on honoring reading and the reader. After students read a book, they sit in a special chair to make a brief presentation about the book, and classmates are encouraged to ask questions, much like in author's chair (see p. 10).

COMMON CORE STATE STANDARDS FOR ENGLISH LANGUAGE ARTS: *BOOK TALKS*
This instructional strategy supports these Common Core State Standards for Reading: Literature and Listening and Speaking:

• Students recount or summarize books they've read.
• Students apply knowledge of the structure and craft of stories.
• Students orally report on a text, often including multimedia components.

Students demonstrate their comprehension as they present book talks.

WHY USE THIS INSTRUCTIONAL STRATEGY

Book talks are motivational. When teachers and students share books, students feel a part of a learning community, and they're much more likely to pick up a book and read it. In addition, when students share a book that they've read and enjoyed, it's a celebratory activity.

HOW TO USE THIS INSTRUCTIONAL STRATEGY

Book talks are informal activities that don't take much time. Teachers regularly introduce books they're adding to the classroom library; otherwise, few students will pick up the book to read. Teachers follow these steps when they use this procedure:

1 **Select a book to share.** Teachers choose a new book to introduce to students or a book that students haven't shown much interest in. They familiarize themselves with the book by reading or rereading it.

2 **Plan a brief presentation.** Teachers plan how they'll introduce the book so students will be interested in reading it. They usually begin by stating the title and author of the book, and they mention the genre or topic and briefly summarize the plot without giving away the ending. Teachers also explain why they liked the book and think about why students might be interested in it. Sometimes they choose a short excerpt to read and an illustration to show.

3 **Present the book talk.** Teachers present the book talk and show the book. They share their excitement about the book and make connections between it and others that students already know about. Their comments are usually enough so that a student will ask to borrow the book to read it.

GO DIGITAL

Podcasts

Students record book talks using a microphone connected to a computer, and then they create digital audio files and publish their performances using a podcast hosting service or post them on the class website. Students identify themselves and state the title of the book they're reviewing and the author's name at the beginning of the podcast. They can also write a brief description or summary to accompany the podcasts.

WHEN TO USE THIS INSTRUCTIONAL STRATEGY

Teachers use book talks to introduce books in the classroom library. At the beginning of the school year, teachers take time to present many of the books, and during the year, they introduce new books that they add to the library. They also talk about the books for a literature circle, or a text set of books for a thematic unit (Gambrell & Almasi, 1996). A second grade teacher might give book talks to introduce these series of easy-to-read books:

- Cynthia Rylant's Henry and Mudge series about a boy and his dog, including *Henry and Mudge and the Big Sleepover* (2007)
- Jane Yolen's sci-fi series, including *Commander Toad and the Big Black Hole* (1996)
- The Magic Tree House series of stories and companion nonfiction books, including *Carnival at Candlelight* (Osborne, 2006)

Or, during a seventh grade unit on the Underground Railroad, teachers might introduce five books about Harriet Tubman and the Underground Railroad and then have students form literature circles to read one of the books.

REFERENCES

Danziger, P. (2006a). *Amber Brown is not a crayon*. New York: Puffin Books.

Danziger, P. (2006b). *You can't eat your chicken pox, Amber Brown*. New York: Puffin Books.

Gambrell, L. B., & Almasi, J. F. (Eds.). (1996). *Lively discussions! Fostering engaged reading*. Newark, DE: International Reading Association.

Osborne, M. P. (2006). *Carnival at candlelight*. New York: Random House.

Robb, L. (2000). *Teaching reading in middle school: A strategic approach to teaching reading that improves comprehension and thinking*. New York: Scholastic.

Rylant, C. (2007). *Henry and Mudge and the big sleepover*. New York: Aladdin Books.

Yolen, J. (1996). *Commander Toad and the big black hole*. New York: Putnam.

7 Choral Reading

Instructional Focus		Grade Levels
☑ Oral Language	☑ Comprehension	☑ PreK–Grade 2
☐ Phonemic Awareness/Phonics	☐ Writing	☑ Grades 3–5
☑ Fluency	☐ Spelling	☐ Grades 6–8
☐ Vocabulary	☐ Content Areas	☑ English Learners

Students read aloud poems, verses, and other texts collaboratively during choral reading. Through multiple readings, students learn to read more expressively and increase their reading fluency. Many arrangements for choral reading are possible: Students may read the text aloud together as a class or divide it and read sections in small groups. Or, individual students may read particular lines or stanzas while the class reads the rest of the text. Here are four possible arrangements:

Echo Reading. A leader reads each line and the group repeats it.

Leader and Chorus Reading. A leader reads the main part of the poem, and the group reads the refrain or chorus in unison.

Small-Group Reading. The class divides into two or more groups, and each group reads aloud one part of the poem.

Cumulative Reading. One student or one group reads the first line or stanza, and another student or group joins in as each line or stanza is read so that a cumulative effect is created.

Students read the text several times, experimenting with different arrangements until they decide which one conveys meaning most effectively.

WHY USE THIS INSTRUCTIONAL STRATEGY

Choral reading provides students, especially struggling readers, with valuable oral reading practice (Rasinski & Padak, 2004). With practice, students become more fluent readers, and when students read more fluently, they're better able to understand what they're reading. Another benefit of choral reading is the shared experience of reading together (Graves, 1992; Larrick, 1991). Students enjoy the camaraderie of reading with their classmates, and less capable readers can join in without embarrassment or fear of failure.

COMMON CORE STATE STANDARDS FOR ENGLISH LANGUAGE ARTS: *CHORAL READING*

This instructional strategy supports these Common Core State Standards for Reading: Literature and Listening and Speaking:

- Students read grade-appropriate poems.
- Students describe how words supply rhythm and meaning in poems.
- Students create engaging audio recordings of poems.

Students learn about the power of language as they participate in choral reading activities.

Scaffolding English Learners

Choral reading is an effective activity for English learners because they practice reading aloud with classmates in a nonthreatening group setting (McCauley & McCauley, 1992). As they read with English-speaking classmates, they hear and practice English pronunciations, phrasing of words in a sentence, and intonation patterns. With practice, students' reading and oral language become more fluent.

HOW TO USE THIS INSTRUCTIONAL STRATEGY

Students work in small groups or together as a class for choral reading activities. Teachers follow this procedure:

1 **Select a poem.** Teachers choose a poem or other text and copy it onto a chart or make multiple copies for students to read.

2 **Arrange the text.** Teachers work with students to decide how to arrange the poem for choral reading. They add marks to the chart, or have students mark individual copies so that they can follow the arrangement.

3 **Rehearse the poem.** Teachers read the poem with students several times at a natural speed, pronouncing words carefully. Many teachers stand so that students can see how they move their mouths to form the words as they read.

4 **Read the poem aloud.** Teachers emphasize that students pronounce words clearly and read with expression. Teachers can tape-record students' reading so that they can hear themselves, and sometimes students want to rearrange the choral reading after hearing an audiotape of their reading.

WHEN TO USE THIS INSTRUCTIONAL STRATEGY

Teachers use choral reading during literature focus units and thematic units or whenever students are reading poems and other short texts with rich language. Choral reading makes students active participants in the poetry experience, and it helps them learn to appreciate the sounds, feelings, and magic of poetry. Many poems can be used for choral reading, and poems with repetitions, echoes, refrains, or questions and answers work well. Try these poems, for example:

"My Parents Think I'm Sleeping," by Jack Prelutsky (2007)

"I Woke Up This Morning," by Karla Kuskin (2003)

"Every Time I Climb a Tree," by David McCord (Paschen, 2005)

"Ode to La Tortilla," by Gary Soto (2005)

"The New Kid on the Block," by Jack Prelutsky (2000)

"Mother to Son," by Langston Hughes (2007)

"A Circle of Sun," by Rebecca Kai Dotlich (Yolen & Peters, 2007)

Poems written specifically for two readers are very effective. Beginning readers enjoy Donald Hall's book-length poem *I Am the Dog/I Am the Cat* (1994), and Paul Fleischman's collection of insect poems, *Joyful Noise: Poems for Two Voices* (2004), works well with older students. Teachers can also use speeches, songs, and longer poems for choral reading. Try, for example, *Brother Eagle, Sister Sky: A Message From Chief Seattle* (Jeffers, 1993), Woody Guthrie's *This Land Is Your Land* (2002), and *The Buck Stops Here: The Presidents of the United States* (Provensen, 1997). For additional books of poetry, check the Booklist on page 20.

BOOKLIST

Poetry Books

Dakos, K. (2002). *The bug in teacher's coffee: And other poems.* New York: HarperCollins. P

Dakos, K. (2004). *Our principal promised to kiss a frog.* New York: Whitman. PM

Giovanni, N. (2008). *Hip hop speaks to children: A celebration of poetry with a beat.* Naperville, IL: Sourcebooks. MU

Martin, B., Jr., & Sampson, M. (2008). *Bill Martin Jr. big book of poetry.* New York: Simon & Schuster. P

Paschen, E., & Raccah, D. (2010). *Poetry speaks who I am: Poems of discovery, inspiration, independence, and everything else.* Naperville, IL: Sourcebooks. U

Prelutsky, J. (Ed.). (2000). *The Random House book of poetry for children.* New York: Random House. PMU

Prelutsky, J. (2005). *It's raining pigs and noodles.* New York: Greenwillow. PM

Prelutsky, J. (2008). *Be glad your nose is on your face and other poems.* New York: Greenwillow. PMU

Vecchione, P. (Ed.). (2002). *Whisper and shout: Poems to memorize.* Chicago: Cricket. MU

Whitehead, J. (2007). *Lunch box mail and other poems.* New York: Henry Holt. PM

P = primary grades (preK–2); M = middle grades (3–5); U = upper grades (6–8)

REFERENCES

Fleischman, P. (2004). *Joyful noise: Poems for two voices.* New York: Harper Trophy.

Graves, D. H. (1992). *Explore poetry.* Portsmouth, NH: Heinemann.

Guthrie, W. (2002). *This land is your land.* Boston: Little, Brown.

Hall, D. (1994). *I am the dog/I am the cat.* New York: Dial Books.

Hughes, L. (2007). *The dream keeper and other poems.* New York: Knopf.

Jeffers, S. (1993). *Brother eagle, sister sky: A message from Chief Seattle.* New York: Puffin Books.

Kuskin, K. (2003). *Moon, have you met my mother? The collected poems of Karla Kuskin.* New York: HarperCollins.

Larrick, N. (1991). *Let's do a poem! Introducing poetry to children.* New York: Delacorte.

McCauley, J. K., & McCauley, D. S. (1992). Using choral reading to promote language learning for ESL students. *The Reading Teacher, 45,* 526–533.

Paschen, E. (Ed.). (2005). *Poetry speaks to children.* Naperville, IL: Sourcebooks MediaFusion.

Prelutsky, J. (2000). *The Random House book of poetry for children.* New York: Random House.

Prelutsky, J. (2007). *My parents think I'm sleeping.* New York: Greenwillow.

Provensen, A. (1997). *The buck stops here: The presidents of the United States.* San Diego: Browndeer Press.

Rasinski, T., & Padak, N. (2004). *Effective reading strategies: Teaching children who find reading difficult.* Upper Saddle River, NJ: Merrill/Prentice Hall.

Soto, G. (2005). *Neighborhood odes.* San Diego: Harcourt.

Yolen, J., & Peters, A. F. (Eds.). (2007). *Here's a little poem.* Cambridge, MA: Candlewick Press.

8 Clusters

Instructional Focus		Grade Levels
☐ Oral Language	☐ Comprehension	☐ PreK–Grade 2
☐ Phonemic Awareness/Phonics	☑ Writing	☑ Grades 3–5
☐ Fluency	☐ Spelling	☑ Grades 6–8
☑ Vocabulary	☑ Content Areas	☑ English Learners

Clusters are spider web–like diagrams drawn on a sheet of paper. Words and phrases are written on rays drawn out from the center circle, and sometimes drawings are used instead of words or to accompany the words (Bromley, 1996; Rico, 2000). Clusters go by several names, including *webs* and *maps*, but whatever the name, they look the same and are used in the same way.

Two kinds of clusters are *unorganized* and *organized clusters*. Unorganized clusters look like a child's drawing of the sun, with many rays drawn out from a center circle. These clusters are most useful for brainstorming equivalent ideas. In contrast, organized clusters are hierarchical: Several rays are drawn out from the center circle, with big ideas listed for each ray. Then more rays with details and examples are added to complete each big idea. The two kinds of clusters are shown on the next page.

WHY USE THIS INSTRUCTIONAL STRATEGY

Clusters are useful because they provide visual representations of ideas; students use these diagrams to brainstorm and organize ideas after reading and before beginning to write (Daniels & Zemelman, 2004). They're more effective than outlines because they're nonlinear and because students like to draw them; in contrast, students often view making outlines as a chore.

Scaffolding English Learners

English learners make clusters using a combination of words and pictures; the visual representation helps them learn how to organize and remember ideas. The words that are written on the clusters are important, too, because they're often unfamiliar words that they're learning or words they need for their writing.

COMMON CORE STATE STANDARDS FOR ENGLISH LANGUAGE ARTS: *CLUSTERS*

This instructional strategy supports these Common Core State Standards for Writing:

- Students use the writing process to develop and revise their compositions.
- Students develop a topic with facts, details, and examples.

Students also make clusters to gather and organize information when they're reading nonfiction texts and content-area textbooks.

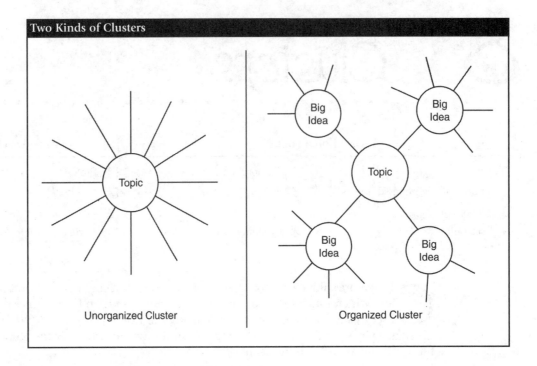

Two Kinds of Clusters

Unorganized Cluster

Organized Cluster

HOW TO USE THIS INSTRUCTIONAL STRATEGY

Students make clusters for a variety of purposes. Sometimes they create a cluster together as a class, and at other times, they make them in small groups or individually. No matter their purpose, students follow these steps:

1 **Select a topic.** Students select a topic and write the word in the center of a circle drawn on a chart or a sheet of paper. The center circle can be in the middle or at the top of the paper.

2 **Design the cluster.** To develop an unorganized cluster, students brainstorm words and phrases that are related to the topic and write them on rays drawn out from the center circle. For an organized cluster, students identify the big ideas, draw a ray from the center circle for each idea, and write the idea's name in a smaller circle at the end of the ray.

3 **Complete the cluster.** For unorganized clusters, students read the words and phrases they've recorded on the cluster and then try to brainstorm additional ideas. To finish an organized cluster, students write details related to each big idea on rays drawn out from each idea circle. Teachers often prompt students to help them think of additional words and phrases.

GO DIGITAL

Inspiration
Students use Inspiration (http://www.inspiration.com) and other online graphics tools to draw clusters and other diagrams. They collect words and images and then organize them hierarchically to create their diagrams. Afterward, they can transform the diagrams into outlines and use them for writing and web-based projects. A simpler version, Kidspiration, is available for children in kindergarten through fifth grade.

WHEN TO USE THIS INSTRUCTIONAL STRATEGY

Clusters can be used in a variety of ways during literature focus units, literature circles, and thematic units (Dymock & Nicholson, 2010). Students use clusters as a tool for learning. For example, they make word clusters—unorganized clusters—and draw out rays for each

A Third Grade Class's Unorganized Cluster

An outer planet - 6th from the sun

You can see Saturn from Earth but you can't see the rings

Temperature is very cold – 285°

10 times as big as the Earth

Saturn's year is 29½ Earth years

Poisonous ball of gas | no life is possible

23 moons

Second largest planet

7 rings made of ice

A Sixth Grader's Organized Cluster

POSEIDON

Who ?
- Ψ God of the sea
- Ψ Romans called him Neptune
- Ψ Second most powerful god
- Ψ Brother of Zeus
- Ψ Married to Amphitrite

What did he do?
- Ψ made tidal waves for his enemies.
- Ψ dried up rivers and lakes of his enemies
- Ψ calmed the storms when he wanted to
- Ψ rode over the sea in a golden chariot
- Ψ invented the horse

What are his symbols?
- Ψ spear called a trident

of the word's meanings, and in learning logs, they make organized clusters of information they're learning about content-area topics, such as clouds and medieval societies. They also make clusters to organize ideas before beginning to write a composition. For a single paragraph, students often use unorganized clusters, but for longer compositions, they use organized clusters in which each big idea represents one paragraph. Students decide which type of cluster they'll make depending on the topic and their purpose for making it.

Students also can make clusters to demonstrate their learning. Instead of writing a report, they create clusters to show what they've learned about a social studies or science topic. For example, students can make a cluster with information about a planet in the solar system, an animal, a state, or a historical event. A third grade class's unorganized cluster about the planet Saturn is shown at the top of page 23. Students also make clusters about a person's life after reading a biography or autobiography. When the clusters are used to demonstrate knowledge, students take more care to spell words correctly, use neater handwriting, and often add drawings, diagrams, and other illustrations, as shown in the sixth grader's organized cluster about Poseidon, the Greek god of the sea, at the bottom of page 23.

REFERENCES

Bromley, K. D. (1996). *Webbing with literature: Creating story maps with children's books.* Boston: Allyn & Bacon.

Daniels, H., & Zemelman, S. (2004). *Subjects matter: Every teacher's guide to content-area reading.* Portsmouth, NH: Heinemann.

Dymock, S., & Nicholson, T. (2010). "High 5!" Strategies to enhance comprehension of expository text. *The Reading Teacher, 64,* 166–178.

Rico, G. L. (2000). *Writing the natural way* (Rev. ed.). Los Angeles: Tarcher.

9 Collaborative Books

Instructional Focus		Grade Levels
☐ Oral Language	☐ Comprehension	☑ PreK–Grade 2
☐ Phonemic Awareness/Phonics	☑ Writing	☑ Grades 3–5
☐ Fluency	☐ Spelling	☐ Grades 6–8
☐ Vocabulary	☑ Content Areas	☑ English Learners

Students work together in small groups to make collaborative books. They each contribute one page or work with a classmate to write a page or a section of the book, and they use the writing process as they draft, revise, and edit their pages. Teachers often make class collaborations with students as a first bookmaking project and to introduce the stages of the writing process. Students write collaborative books to retell a favorite story, illustrate a poem with one line or a stanza on each page, or write an informational book or biography. Alphabet books (see p. 4) are also collaborative books.

WHY USE THIS INSTRUCTIONAL STRATEGY

The benefit of collaborative books is that students share the work so that books are completed much more quickly and easily than individual books (Tompkins, 2012). Because students write only one page or section, it takes less time for teachers to conference with them and assist them with time-consuming revising and editing.

Scaffolding English Learners

English learners are more likely to be successful when they write books collaboratively than when they write independently because they work with their English-speaking classmates who provide assistance on choosing vocabulary, phrasing sentences and paragraphs, and spelling English words.

COMMON CORE STATE STANDARDS FOR ENGLISH LANGUAGE ARTS: *COLLABORATIVE BOOKS*

This instructional strategy supports these Common Core State Standards for Writing:

- Students write informative texts to examine a topic.
- Students use the writing process to plan, revise, and edit their writing.

Students demonstrate their ability to develop a topic with facts, details, and examples as they create pages for collaborative books.

HOW TO USE THIS INSTRUCTIONAL STRATEGY

Students work together as a class or in small groups to write collaborative books. Teachers follow this procedure:

1 Choose a topic. Teachers choose a broad topic related to a literature focus unit or thematic unit. Then students narrow the broad topic or choose a specific topic for their page.

2 Introduce the page or section design. If students are each contributing one page for a class informational book on penguins, for example, they choose a fact or other piece of information about penguins to write. They might draw a picture related to the fact at the top of the page and write the fact underneath it. Teachers often model the procedure by writing one page of the book together as a class before students begin working on their pages.

3 Make rough drafts. Students share the pages in revising groups (see p. 116), and they revise their pictures and text after getting feedback from classmates. Then students correct mechanical errors and make the final copy of their pages.

4 Compile the pages. Students add a title page and covers. Older students might also prepare a table of contents, an introduction, and a conclusion, and add a bibliography at the end. To make the book sturdier, teachers often laminate the covers (or all pages in the book) and have the book bound.

5 Make copies of the book. Teachers often make copies of the book for each student. The specially bound copy is often placed in the class or school library.

WHEN TO USE THIS INSTRUCTIONAL STRATEGY

As part of literature focus units, students often retell a story or create an innovation, or new version of a story, in a collaborative book. They can also retell a chapter-book story by having each student retell one chapter of the story. Students also can illustrate a poem or song by writing one line or stanza on each page and then drawing or painting an illustration. *The Lady With the Alligator Purse* (Hoberman, 2003), *There Was an Old lady Who Swallowed a Fly* (Taback, 1997), *Cats Sleep Anywhere* (Farjeon, 1999), and *America the Beautiful* (Bates, 2003) are four examples of song and poem retellings that have been published as picture books; these books can be used as examples for students to examine before they write their own retellings.

Students also write informational books and biographies collaboratively. For informational books, students each write a page with one fact, and for biographies, they each write about one event in the person's life. A page from a first grade class book about Johnny Appleseed, written as part of a unit on apples, is shown on the next page. After the first graders wrote rough drafts, they worked with an upper grade student to type and print out final copies of their texts.

Students can use this approach to write collaborative reports, too. They work in small groups or with a partner to research a topic related to a thematic unit. Students often use a cluster (see p. 21) or data chart (see p. 31) to record the information they learn, then they write one section of the report using information they learned through their research. They continue the writing process to revise and edit their writing. Last, they make a final copy and add their section to the class book.

A Page From a First Grade Class Book

Johnny Appleseed is leaving home. He is walking on his way to the Ohio Valley. He took a sack of apple seeds and the hat on his head is really a pot. He cooks in it. He took a Bible to read and he has a stick in his hand. He has no more clothes.

REFERENCES

Bates, K. L. (2003). *America the beautiful.* New York: Putnam.

Farjeon, E. (1999). *Cats sleep anywhere.* New York: HarperCollins.

Hoberman, M. A. (2003). *The lady with the alligator purse.* Boston: Little, Brown.

Taback, S. (1997). *There was an old lady who swallowed a fly.* New York: Viking.

Tompkins, G. E. (2012). *Teaching writing: Balancing process and product* (6th ed.). Boston: Pearson.

10 Cubing

Instructional Focus

☐ Oral Language	☑ Comprehension
☐ Phonemic Awareness/Phonics	☑ Writing
☐ Fluency	☐ Spelling
☐ Vocabulary	☑ Content Areas

Grade Levels

☐ PreK–Grade 2
☐ Grades 3–5
☑ Grades 6–8
☑ English Learners

Students explore a topic from six dimensions or viewpoints when they do a cubing (Axelrod & Cooper, 2009; Neeld, 1990). The name "cubing" comes from the fact that cubes have six sides, just as there are six dimensions in this instructional procedure. These are the six dimensions:

Describe. Students describe the topic, including its colors, shapes, and sizes.

Compare. Students compare the topic to something else, explaining how it's similar to or different from this other thing.

Associate. Students associate the topic with something else and explain why it makes them think of this other thing.

Analyze. Students analyze the topic and tell how it's made or what it's composed of.

Apply. Students apply the topic, describing how it can be used or what can be done with it.

Argue For or Against. Students take a stand and argue for or against the topic, giving reasons to support their position.

Cubes can be used in two ways: Students can create cubes to review a topic they've been studying, or they can create cubes as projects to demonstrate what they've learned during a thematic unit. The first way is less formal and focuses on using cubing as a tool for learning; the second way is more formal, and students use the writing process to draft, revise, and edit their writing for each side of the cube.

WHY USE THIS INSTRUCTIONAL STRATEGY

Cubing is a valuable instructional strategy because students use higher level thinking processes as they create a cube, and they share their sophisticated thinking with classmates

COMMON CORE STATE STANDARDS FOR ENGLISH LANGUAGE ARTS: *CUBING*

This instructional strategy supports these Common Core State Standards for Reading: Informational Text and Writing:

- Students analyze texts, citing evidence, drawing inferences, and determining the author's viewpoint.
- Students draw on information from multiple sources.
- Students write explanations, summaries, and arguments.

Students integrate knowledge and ideas as they explore topics and create cubes.

as they work together in small groups. As students craft paragraphs for each side of the cube, they further refine their thinking and deepen their understanding of the topic.

Scaffolding English Learners

You might think that cubing is too difficult for English learners, but this instructional strategy embodies the qualities of effective instruction for students who are learning English (Akhavan, 2006). It's an authentic activity: Students work collaboratively in small groups, they're actively involved in the content they're learning, and they create visuals to support their learning.

HOW TO USE THIS INSTRUCTIONAL STRATEGY

Students work together in small groups to create cubes, and teachers follow these steps as they implement this procedure:

1 **Choose a topic.** Students choose a familiar topic to cube.

2 **Divide students into groups.** Students work in six small groups; each group examines the topic from one dimension. As an alternative, teachers divide students into six-member groups and have each group cube the topic; each member in each group will examine the topic from one dimension, and the group will create a cube.

3 **Brainstorm.** Students brainstorm ideas about the dimension and then quickwrite (see p. 99) or make a drawing using the ideas they gathered.

4 **Complete the cube.** Students share their quickwrites with the class and then attach them to the sides of a box. They can also construct a cube by folding and gluing cardboard or paper into a six-sided box.

WHEN TO USE THIS INSTRUCTIONAL STRATEGY

Cubing is a useful procedure for examining topics related to thematic units; fifth through eighth graders can cube topics such as Antarctica, the United States Constitution, endangered animals, the Underground Railroad, and the Nile River. Students can also use cubing to explore a character in a story. Fox example, a small group of fifth graders did this cubing about Annemarie, the Christian girl who hides her Jewish friend, Ellen, in *Number the Stars* (Lowry, 2011):

Describe: Annemarie is ten years old. She is Danish and a Christian. She has silvery blond hair and blue eyes. She is smart, athletic, and a good friend to Ellen.

Compare: Annemarie is a lot like her friend Ellen. They are both Danish girls. They are both good students and good friends but they look different. Annemarie has blond hair and Ellen has brown hair. Annemarie is skinnier than Ellen and she is a better runner than Ellen. But the biggest difference is religion and what that means during World War II. Annemarie is safe because she is a Christian but Ellen is in great danger just because she is Jewish and the Germans wanted to get rid of all the Jews.

Associate: Annemarie is a lot like us. We would like her if she was in our class.

Analyze: Annemarie is just a normal girl, but she has to do some dangerous things because of the war. If there was a war in America, we might have to do dangerous things, too. We would have to be as brave as she is.

Apply: When we read about Annemarie, we learned a lot about being brave. We learned that you can't be selfish and you have to think about others. You also have to be smart and one way to be smart is to pretend to be dumb. It is better not to know too many secrets during a war.

Argue: Annemarie is the bravest person we know. She just wanted to be a girl but she had to take a stand. Ellen was brave, too, but she didn't have any choice. She would have to go to a concentration camp and probably die if she wasn't brave. Annemarie was different. She could have closed her eyes and not helped her friend, but she didn't do that because she is so brave. She made the very important choice to be brave.

This cubing about Annemarie and Ellen shows how students deepen their understanding of a story as they think about it from each of the six dimensions.

REFERENCES

Akhavan, N. (2006). *Help! My kids don't all speak English: How to set up a language workshop in your linguistically diverse classroom.* Portsmouth, NH: Heinemann.

Axelrod, R. B., & Cooper, C. R. (2009). *Axelrod and Cooper's concise guide to writing* (5th ed.). New York: St. Martin's Press.

Lowry, L. (2011). *Number the stars.* New York: Sandpiper.

Neeld, E. C. (1990). *Writing* (3rd ed.). Upper Saddle River, NJ: Scott Foresman/Pearson.

11 Data Charts

Instructional Focus		Grade Levels
☐ Oral Language	☑ Comprehension	☑ PreK–Grade 2
☐ Phonemic Awareness/Phonics	☑ Writing	☑ Grades 3–5
☐ Fluency	☐ Spelling	☑ Grades 6–8
☐ Vocabulary	☑ Content Areas	☑ English Learners

Data charts are grids that students make and use as a tool for organizing information about a topic (McKenzie, 1979). Grids are best suited for topics that can be divided into four or more subtopics. In literature focus units, data charts can be used to compare information about versions of folktales and fairy tales, such as "Cinderella" stories, or a collection of books by an author, such as Eric Carle, Chris Van Allsburg, or Gary Paulsen. In thematic units, data charts can be used to record information about a big idea, such as the solar system or Native American tribes. Students also use data charts as a prewriting activity, to collect and organize information for a report or an essay (McMackin & Siegel, 2002).

WHY USE THIS INSTRUCTIONAL STRATEGY

This instructional strategy is very useful when students need to organize information about a topic, either after reading or before writing (Readence, Moore, & Rickelman, 2000). Students think about the information they're collecting and then create a data chart that fits the topic. This process of analyzing a topic contributes to students' understanding of the topic.

HOW TO USE THIS INSTRUCTIONAL STRATEGY

Teachers use this instructional strategy with the whole class or small groups, and individual students can also create their own data charts. Here are the steps in the procedure:

1 **Design the data chart.** Teachers or students choose a topic and decide how to set up the data chart: Characteristics of the topic will be listed across the top of the chart and examples in the left column.

COMMON CORE STATE STANDARDS FOR ENGLISH LANGUAGE ARTS: *DATA CHARTS*

This instructional strategy supports these Common Core State Standards for Reading: Informational Text and Writing:

- Students conduct research projects.
- Students draw information from multiple print and digital sources.
- Students use the writing process to plan, revise, and edit their compositions.

Students use data charts as a tool when they're conducting research.

2 **Draw the chart.** Teachers or students create a skeleton chart that fits the topic on butcher paper or on a sheet of paper. They write the characteristics across the top and the examples in the left column.

3 **Complete the chart.** Students complete the chart by adding words, pictures, sentences, or paragraphs in each cell. Sometimes it's necessary to redesign the chart to accommodate new information that's uncovered.

WHEN TO USE THIS INSTRUCTIONAL STRATEGY

Students use data charts during literature focus units and thematic units; they often start the chart at the beginning of the unit and then add information to it as they read books or learn more about the topic. An excerpt from a data chart that a fifth grade class developed during a unit on whales is shown here. Small groups of students added information about the different types of whales to a large class chart, and then students used the class chart as a resource in developing individual data charts in their learning logs.

Excerpt From a Fifth Grade Class Data Chart

Whales

Kind	Looks	Food	Baleen or Teeth	Live
Blue Whale	largest animal 100' long blue diatoms – yellow plants on his belly	Krill	B	all oceans very rare
Narwals	10–15' gray – top white – belly dark spots all over	fish squid	T	Arctic Ocean
Humpback Whales	50' long flippers black – top white – belly warts no hump!	krill and fish	B	all oceans

Alternatively, students can develop a data chart in small groups or together as a class as a review at the end of a unit. Another possibility is that students develop a data chart as a project at the end of a unit to summarize their learning. Teachers can create a data chart on a bulletin board or a classroom wall. Then students divide into small groups to focus on a particular example; they write information on sheets of paper and then add them to complete the row for their example.

REFERENCES

McKenzie, G. R. (1979). Data charts: A crutch for helping pupils organize reports. *Language Arts, 56,* 784–788.

McMackin, M. C., & Siegel, B. S. (2002). *Knowing how: Researching and writing nonfiction 3–8.* Portland, ME: Stenhouse.

Readence, J. E., Moore, D. W., & Rickelman, R. J. (2000). *Prereading activities for content area reading and learning* (3rd ed.). Newark, DE: International Reading Association.

12   Double-Entry Journals

Instructional Focus		Grade Levels
☐ Oral Language	☑ Comprehension	☐ PreK–Grade 2
☐ Phonemic Awareness/Phonics	☑ Writing	☑ Grades 3–5
☐ Fluency	☐ Spelling	☑ Grades 6–8
☐ Vocabulary	☑ Content Areas	☐ English Learners

A double-entry journal is a special type of reading log in which the pages are divided into two columns; students write different types of information in each column (Barone, 1990; Berthoff, 1981). In the left column, students write quotes from the story, nonfiction book, or content-area textbook they're reading, and in the right column, they reflect on each quote. They may relate a quote to their own background knowledge, react to it, write a question, or make some other connection. Excerpts from a fifth grader's double-entry journal about C. S. Lewis's classic story, *The Lion, the Witch and the Wardrobe* (2005), are shown on the next page.

WHY USE THIS INSTRUCTIONAL STRATEGY

Teachers use double-entry journals to help students structure their thinking about a text they're reading (Tovani, 2000). The quotes that students select show what they think is important about the text, and the types of responses they make in the right column reveal their understanding of what they've read.

HOW TO USE THIS INSTRUCTIONAL STRATEGY

Students usually write double-entry journals independently after they read each chapter or two of a novel or nonfiction book, or a chapter in a content-area textbook. They follow these steps:

1   **Design journal pages.** Students divide the pages in their reading logs into two columns. They may label the left column "Quotes" and the right column "Comments" or "Reflections."

COMMON CORE STATE STANDARDS FOR ENGLISH LANGUAGE ARTS: *DOUBLE-ENTRY JOURNALS*

This instructional strategy supports these Common Core State Standards for Reading: Literature:

- Students explain what a text quote says and draw inferences from it.
- Students use textual evidence to support their story analysis.
- Students analyze how dialogue and events influence a story's development.

Students apply their knowledge about literature in double-entry journals.

Excerpts From a Fifth Grader's Double-Entry Journal	
Quotes	Reflections
Chapter 1 I tell you this is the sort of house where no one is going to mind what we do.	I remember the time that I went to Beaumont, Texas to stay with my aunt. My aunt's house was very large. She had a piano and she let us play it. She told us what we could do whatever we wanted to.
Chapter 5 "How do you know?" he asked, "that your sister's story is not true?"	It reminds me of when I was little and I had an imaginary place. I would go there in my mind. I made up all kinds of make-believe stories about myself in this imaginary place. One time I told my big brother about my imaginary place. He laughed at me and told me I was silly. But it didn't bother me because nobody can stop me from thinking what I want.
Chapter 15 Still they could see the shape of the great lion lying dead in his bonds.	When Aslan died I thought about when my Uncle Carl died.
They're nibbling at the cords.	This reminds me of the story where the lion lets the mouse go and the mouse helps the lion.

2   **Copy quotes into journals.** As students read or immediately afterward, they copy one or more important or interesting quotes in the left column of their reading logs.

3   **Reflect on the quotes.** Students reread the quotes and in the right column explain their reasons for choosing the quote and what it means to them. Sometimes it's easier if students share the quotes with a reading buddy or in a grand conversation (see p. 45) before they complete the right column.

WHEN TO USE THIS INSTRUCTIONAL STRATEGY

Teachers have students write in double-entry journals in place of other types of reading logs when students are reading novels during literature focus units and literature circles. Sometimes teachers change the headings for the two columns. For example, instead of recording quotes from the story, students can write "Reading Notes" in the left column and then add "Connections" in the right column; in the left column, they summarize their reading, and then in the right column, they make connections to the events. In addition, younger students use the double-entry format for prediction journals (Macon, Bewell, & Vogt, 1991). They label the columns "Predictions" and "What Really Happened." In the left column, they write or draw a picture of what they predict will happen in the story before reading it. Then afterward, they draw or write what actually happened in the right column.

Students also use double-entry journals to take notes when they're reading nonfiction books and content-area textbooks. They identify the big ideas and summarize them in the left-side "Notes" column and then comment on the significance of the ideas in the right-side "Reflections" column (Daniels & Zemelman, 2004). As with double-entry journals used with stories, it's the right column that's particularly valuable because students have an opportunity to think more deeply about the big ideas they're reading.

REFERENCES

Barone, D. (1990). The written responses of young children: Beyond comprehension to story understanding. *The New Advocate, 3,* 49–56.

Berthoff, A. E. (1981). *The making of meaning.* Montclair, NJ: Boynton/Cook.

Daniels, H., & Zemelman, S. (2004). *Subjects matter: Every teacher's guide to content-area reading.* Portsmouth, NH: Heinemann.

Lewis, C. S. (2005). *The lion, the witch and the wardrobe.* New York: HarperCollins.

Macon, J. M., Bewell, D., & Vogt, M. E. (1991). *Responses to literature: Grades K–8.* Newark, DE: International Reading Association.

Tovani, C. (2000). *I read it, but I don't get it: Comprehension strategies for adolescent readers.* York, ME: Stenhouse.

13 Exclusion Brainstorming

Instructional Focus		Grade Levels
☐ Oral Language	☑ Comprehension	☐ PreK–Grade 2
☐ Phonemic Awareness/Phonics	☐ Writing	☑ Grades 3–5
☐ Fluency	☐ Spelling	☑ Grades 6–8
☑ Vocabulary	☑ Content Areas	☑ English Learners

Teachers use exclusion brainstorming to activate students' background knowledge and expand their understanding about a social studies or science topic before reading (Blachowicz & Fisher, 2010). They present students with a list of words to read, and students identify the words on the list that relate to the topic as well as those that don't belong. Then after reading, students review the list of words and decide whether they chose the words correctly.

WHY USE THIS INSTRUCTIONAL STRATEGY

Exclusion brainstorming is a useful prereading activity because as students talk about the words on the word list and try to decide which ones are related, they expand their background knowledge, gain experience with key vocabulary words, and develop a purpose for reading (Wormeli, 2001).

HOW TO USE THIS INSTRUCTIONAL STRATEGY

Exclusion brainstorming is a whole-class activity because students benefit from listening to classmates and the teacher talk about the words in the word list. Once students are familiar with the instructional strategy, they sometimes work in small groups and then share their lists with the class. Students work together as a class or in small groups for this instructional strategy. Teachers follow this procedure:

1 **Prepare a word list.** Teachers identify words related to a nonfiction book or content-area textbook chapter that students will read and include a few words that don't fit with the topic. They write the list on the whiteboard or on an overhead transparency, or they make copies for students.

COMMON CORE STATE STANDARDS FOR ENGLISH LANGUAGE ARTS: *EXCLUSION BRAINSTORMING*

This instructional strategy supports these Common Core State Standards for Reading: Informational Text and Language:

- Students draw on information from background knowledge and multiple print and digital sources.
- Students determine the meaning of academic vocabulary in grade-appropriate texts.

Students integrate knowledge and vocabulary as they participate in exclusion brainstorming activities.

2 **Read the list with students.** Then, in small groups or together as a class, students decide which words are related to the text and which ones aren't. They draw circles around words that they think aren't related.

3 **Learn about the topic.** Students read the assignment, noticing whether the words in the exclusion brainstorming exercise are mentioned in the text.

4 **Check the list.** After reading, students check their exclusion brainstorming list and make corrections based on their reading. They put checkmarks by related words and cross out unrelated words, whether they circled them earlier or not.

WHEN TO USE THIS INSTRUCTIONAL STRATEGY

Teachers use exclusion brainstorming as a prereading activity to familiarize students with key concepts and vocabulary before they read nonfiction books and articles. An eighth grade teacher, for example, prepared the following list of words before his students read an article on the Arctic Ocean; all of the words except *penguins*, *South Pole*, and *precipitation* were related to the Arctic Ocean. Students circled seven words as possibly unrelated, and after reading, they crossed out the same three words that their teacher expected them to eliminate.

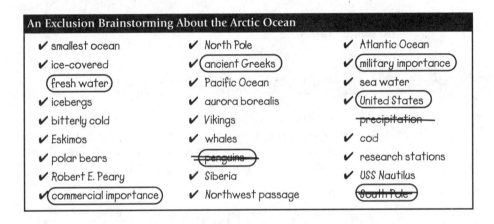

An Exclusion Brainstorming About the Arctic Ocean

✔ smallest ocean	✔ North Pole	✔ Atlantic Ocean
✔ ice-covered	✔ (ancient Greeks)	✔ (military importance)
(fresh water)	✔ Pacific Ocean	✔ sea water
✔ icebergs	✔ aurora borealis	✔ (United States)
✔ bitterly cold	✔ Vikings	~~precipitation~~
✔ Eskimos	✔ whales	✔ cod
✔ polar bears	~~(penguins)~~	✔ research stations
✔ Robert E. Peary	✔ Siberia	✔ USS Nautilus
✔(commercial importance)	✔ Northwest passage	~~(South Pole)~~

Exclusion brainstorming can also be used with novels when teachers want to focus beforehand on a social studies or science concept. A fourth grade teacher created the exclusion brainstorming list shown on the next page before reading *The Ballad of Lucy Whipple* (Cushman, 1998), the story of a young girl who travels with her family to California during the gold rush. The teacher used this activity to introduce vocabulary words and to help students develop an understanding of life during the California gold rush. Students circled seven words before reading; after reading, they crossed out three words, all different from the ones they had circled earlier.

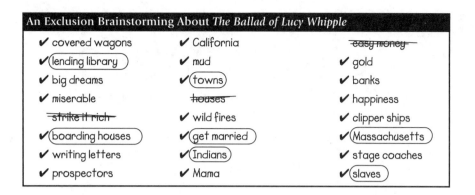

An Exclusion Brainstorming About *The Ballad of Lucy Whipple*

✔ covered wagons	✔ California	~~easy money~~
✔ (lending library)	✔ mud	✔ gold
✔ big dreams	✔ (towns)	✔ banks
✔ miserable	~~houses~~	✔ happiness
~~strike it rich~~	✔ wild fires	✔ clipper ships
✔ (boarding houses)	✔ (get married)	✔ (Massachusetts)
✔ writing letters	✔ (Indians)	✔ stage coaches
✔ prospectors	✔ Mama	✔ (slaves)

REFERENCES

Blachowicz, C., & Fisher, P. J. (2010). *Teaching vocabulary in all classrooms* (4th ed.). Boston: Pearson.

Cushman, K. (1998). *The ballad of Lucy Whipple*. New York: HarperCollins.

Wormeli, R. (2001). *Meet me in the middle: Becoming an accomplished middle-level teacher*. Portland, ME: Stenhouse.

14 Gallery Walks

Instructional Focus		Grade Levels
☐ Oral Language	☐ Comprehension	☐ PreK–Grade 2
☐ Phonemic Awareness/Phonics	☑ Writing	☑ Grades 3–5
☐ Fluency	☐ Spelling	☑ Grades 6–8
☐ Vocabulary	☑ Content Areas	☐ English Learners

Students move around the classroom during a gallery walk to view, read, and respond to classmates' writing and multimedia projects. The work is displayed on the walls around the classroom or placed on students' desks. Classmates respond by writing comments and questions on little self-stick notes and attaching them to the edge of the student's work or by writing comments on a "graffiti board" (a sheet of paper) posted next to each student's work. Fifth graders, for example, view classmates' maps of the American colonies or clusters they've made about a state, sixth graders share idiom posters with literal and figurative meanings that they've created, and eighth graders read copies of letters to the editor of the local newspaper that classmates have written and already sent to the newspaper office.

Students' work can be completed or in progress. When the work has been completed, a gallery walk is a celebration, much like the author's chair (see p. 10). For example, third graders set books they've published during writing workshop on their desks; classmates move around the classroom, stopping at each student's desk to read the book. When the work is in progress, a gallery walk functions much like a revising group (see p. 116) to provide feedback and suggestions to authors. For example, sixth graders post copies of drafts of poems for classmates to read and highlight favorite lines in them.

WHY USE THIS INSTRUCTIONAL STRATEGY

A gallery walk provides an immediate audience for students' writing, multigenre, and multimedia projects (Bergen, 2005). The activity can be completed much more quickly than if each student were to share his or her work in front of the class, and because classmates will view their work, students are more motivated than when the teacher's the only audience. In addition, students provide supportive feedback through their responses to their classmates, and they learn new ideas they can incorporate in their own projects.

COMMON CORE STATE STANDARDS FOR ENGLISH LANGUAGE ARTS: *GALLERY WALKS*

This instructional strategy supports these Common Core State Standards for Writing and Language:

• Students use the writing process to revise and edit their writing and get feedback from classmates.
• Students demonstrate grade-appropriate use of Standard English conventions, including spelling.

Students share their compositions with a variety of audiences through gallery walks.

HOW TO USE THIS INSTRUCTIONAL STRATEGY

A gallery walk is a whole-class activity. Teachers follow these steps as they implement this procedure:

1 Display the work. Students and the teacher post the work on classroom walls or place it on desks in preparation for the gallery walk.

2 Provide comment sheets. Teachers give students self-stick notes on which to write comments or place graffiti sheets next to each student's work.

3 Give directions for the gallery walk. Teachers explain the purpose of the gallery walk, how to view and/or read the work, and what types of comments to make to classmates. Teachers also set time limits and direct students to visit three, five, eight, or more students' work, if there isn't time to see everyone's work.

4 Model how to view, read, and respond. Teachers model how to behave during the gallery walk, using one or two students' work as examples.

5 Direct the flow of traffic. Teachers direct students as they move around the classroom, making sure that all students' work is viewed, read, and responded to and that comments are supportive and useful.

6 Bring closure to the gallery walk. Teachers ask students to move to their own projects and look at the comments, questions, or other responses they've received. Often one or two students share their responses or comment on the gallery walk experience.

WHEN TO USE THIS INSTRUCTIONAL STRATEGY

A good way to introduce a gallery walk is to post photos and have students move around the classroom, writing what the picture makes them think of on self-stick notes, which they attach under the picture. This first experience isn't threatening because students' work isn't being critiqued, but after this experience, students are more prepared to respond to classmates' writing and media productions. After students learn to make positive, supportive comments about classmates' work, they can also try writing questions after reading classmates' rough drafts to assist them in revising their writing. Students read the rough drafts and then write questions asking classmates to clarify, rephrase, or extend an idea. For example, after reading a fourth grader's rough draft report about volcanoes, students asked these questions:

What does *magma* mean?

Are there any volcanoes in California?

Can you add *first*, *second*, and *third* for the sequence?

What's your title?

Are mountains and volcanoes the same thing?

What starts the fire in the volcano?

Are any volcanoes exploding today?

Questions like these provide direction for students as they revise their writing.

GO DIGITAL

Wikis
Students showcase their writing, even multimedia projects, on classroom wikis, and classmates and parents can view and comment on the writing. Wikis—the name comes from the Hawaiian word for *quick*—work well for online gallery walks because they're safe publication sites with privacy controls. Only members can view students' work and submit comments.

REFERENCE

Bergen, S. (2005). Gallery walk of questions: Asking questions to think critically. In G. E. Tompkins & C. Blanchfield (Eds.), *50 ways to develop strategic writers* (pp. 53–55). Upper Saddle River, NJ: Merrill/Prentice Hall.

15 Goldilocks Strategy

Instructional Focus			Grade Levels
☐ Oral Language	☑ Comprehension		☑ PreK–Grade 2
☐ Phonemic Awareness/Phonics	☐ Writing		☑ Grades 3–5
☑ Fluency	☐ Spelling		☐ Grades 6–8
☐ Vocabulary	☐ Content Areas		☑ English Learners

Students use the Goldilocks Strategy (Ohlhausen & Jepsen, 1992) to select books to read independently. Goldilocks in "The Three Bears" folktale classified the porridge as "too hot," "too cold," and "just right"; similarly, books that students read can be categorized as "too hard," "too easy," or "just right." Books in the "too hard" category include those that are confusing and have many unfamiliar words, small type, and few illustrations; "too easy" books are ones that students have read before or can read fluently; and "just right" books are interesting, with a few unfamiliar words. The books in each category vary according to each student's reading level.

Students at any grade level can use the Goldilocks Strategy because of the way the characteristics are stated. A third grade class developed the Goldilocks Strategy chart shown on the next page, but the characteristics might be worded differently by students at other grade levels.

WHY USE THIS INSTRUCTIONAL STRATEGY

When students learn to use the Goldilocks Strategy, they can choose books at their own reading level and assume more responsibility for choosing books for reading workshop or another independent reading time. In addition, they're likely to read more and to enjoy reading more than those students who don't choose books at an appropriate level of difficulty or who are assigned books to read.

HOW TO USE THIS INSTRUCTIONAL STRATEGY

Teachers introduce the Goldilocks Strategy and explain how students should choose books for independent reading. The students develop a chart to refer to as they choose books that are "just right" for them. The procedure involves these steps:

COMMON CORE STATE STANDARDS FOR ENGLISH LANGUAGE ARTS: *GOLDILOCKS STRATEGY*

This instructional strategy supports these Common Core State Standards for Reading: Literature, Reading: Informational Text, and Reading: Foundational Skills:

- Students read grade-appropriate stories, poems, and nonfiction books.
- Students read with sufficient fluency to support comprehension.

As students read "just right" books, they grow as readers so they can read grade-level texts.

A Third Grade Class Chart on the Goldilocks Strategy

How to Choose the Best Books for YOU

"Too Easy" Books

1. The book is short.
2. The print is big.
3. You have read the book before.
4. You know all the words in the book.
5. The book has a lot of pictures.
6. You are an expert on this topic.

"Just Right" Books

1. The book looks interesting.
2. You can decode most of the words in the book.
3. Mrs. Donnelly has read this book aloud to you.
4. You have read other books by this author.
5. There's someone to give you help if you need it.
6. You know something about this topic.

"Too Hard" Books

1. The book is long.
2. The print is small.
3. There aren't many pictures in the book.
4. There are a lot of words that you can't decode.
5. There's no one to help you read this book.
6. You don't know much about this topic.

1 Introduce the Goldilocks Strategy. Teachers explain that the Goldilocks Strategy is a procedure students use to select books during reading workshop. They share three books with students and talk about the books they like to read themselves. They share a book that's too easy for them (e.g., a book written for young children), a book that's too hard (e. g., an automotive repair book, directions for knitting a sweater, or a college textbook), and a book that's just right (e.g., a novel). Teachers emphasize that everyone has books that fit into these three categories.

2 Analyze books. Teachers talk with students about the books that are too easy, too hard, and just right for them, and students identify some of the characteristics of each type. Next, teachers create a class chart with students listing the characteristics of books that are too hard, too easy, and just right. They post the chart in the classroom library center and encourage students to use the strategy when selecting books.

3 Apply the strategy. Teachers ask students to use the three categories when they discuss books they're reading.

WHEN TO USE THIS INSTRUCTIONAL STRATEGY

Students use these three categories as they select books in the classroom library and the school library for reading workshop and other independent reading times. They also use the categories in conferences with the teacher to talk about the books they're reading. For example, a second grader was flipping through the pages of *Tales of a Fourth Grade Nothing* (Blume, 2007) during reading workshop, and her teacher asked if she was enjoying the book. The girl responded, "I think this is too hard. My sister just read it and she said it was really good. But I just know some of the words—like *television*. It's a big word but I know it. I guess it is a 'too hard' book, but I wanted to read it." And, a seventh grader said this during a conference with his teacher: "I just finished rereading this book—*Hatchet* [Paulsen, 2007]. We read it in Mr. Dodd's class last year and when I saw it on the shelf, I just wanted to read it again. I guess you could call it a 'too easy' book because I had read it before and it wasn't hard for me to read, but it was good and I liked it even better this time." Students can also code the books in their reading logs (see p. 113) according to the three categories using the initials TH for "too hard," TE for "too easy," and JR for "just right."

REFERENCES

Blume, J. (2007). *Tales of a fourth grade nothing*. New York: Puffin Books.

Ohlhausen, M. M., & Jepsen, M. (1992). Lessons from Goldilocks: "Someone has been choosing my books but I can make my own choices now!" *The New Advocate*, 5, 31–46.

Paulsen, G. (2007). *Hatchet*. New York: Simon & Schuster.

16 Grand Conversations

Instructional Focus		Grade Levels
☑ Oral Language	☑ Comprehension	☑ PreK–Grade 2
☐ Phonemic Awareness/Phonics	☐ Writing	☑ Grades 3–5
☐ Fluency	☐ Spelling	☑ Grades 6–8
☐ Vocabulary	☐ Content Areas	☐ English Learners

A grand conversation is a discussion about a story in which students explore the big ideas and reflect on their feelings (Peterson & Eeds, 2007). They're different than traditional discussions because they're student centered. In these discussions, students take responsibility for their own learning and do most of the talking as they voice their opinions and support their views with examples from the story. They talk about what puzzles them, what they find interesting, their personal connections to the story, connections to the world, and connections they notice between this story and others they've read. Students usually don't raise their hands to be called on; instead, they take turns and speak when no one else is speaking, much as adults do when they talk with friends. Students also encourage their classmates to contribute to the conversation. Even though teachers sit in on grand conversations, the talk is primarily among the students.

Grand conversations have two parts. The first part is open ended: Students talk about their reactions to the book, and their comments determine the direction of the conversation; teachers share their responses, ask questions, and provide information. Later in the grand conversations, teachers focus students' attention on one or two aspects of the book that they didn't talk about in the first part of the conversation. For English learners to participate successfully in grand conversations, they need to feel comfortable and safe in the group (Graves & Fitzgerald, 2003).

Martinez and Roser (1995) researched the content of students' grand conversations, and they found that students often talk about story events and characters or explore the themes of the stories but delve less often into the author's craft to explore the way he or she structured the story, the arrangement of text and illustrations on the page, or the author's use of figurative or repetitive language. The researchers called these three directions that conversations can take *experience*, *message*, and *object*.

Drawing students' attention to the "object" is important because they apply what they've learned about the author's craft when they write their own stories. Students who know more about leads, pacing, figurative language, point of view, imagery, surprise endings, voice, and flashbacks write better stories than those who don't. One way teachers help

---

COMMON CORE STATE STANDARDS FOR ENGLISH LANGUAGE ARTS: *GRAND CONVERSATIONS*

This instructional strategy supports these Common Core State Standards for Reading: Literature and Speaking and Listening:

- Students engage in discussions, building on classmates' ideas and expressing their own clearly.
- Students cite textual evidence to support their understanding.
- Students analyze theme and other elements of story structure.

Students participate in grand conversations to deepen their comprehension of grade-appropriate stories.

students examine the author's craft is through the questions they ask during grand conversations. For example, teachers ask students to think about why Kate DiCamillo directs comments to the readers in *The Tale of Despereaux* (2006) and the way Paul Fleischman features a different character's viewpoint in each chapter of *Seedfolks* (2004).

The stories you choose to share with students matter, too. Martinez and Roser (1995) notice that some books lend themselves to talk about "message" and others to talk about "experience" or "object." Stories with dramatic plots or those that present a problem students can relate to, such as *Chrysanthemum* (Henkes, 1996) and *Jeremy Thatcher, Dragon Hatcher* (Coville, 2002), focus the conversation on the book as "experience." Multilayered stories or books in which main characters deal with dilemmas, such as *Smoky Night* (Bunting, 1999) and *Princess Academy* (Hale, 2007), focus the conversation on the "message." Books with distinctive structures or language features, such as *Flotsam* (Wiesner, 2006), focus the conversation on the "object."

WHY USE THIS INSTRUCTIONAL STRATEGY

Participating in grand conversations helps students deepen their comprehension of a story and motivates them to continue reading. The social aspect of grand conversations appeals to many students, and others appreciate these discussions because their classmates and the teacher clarify their confusions so that they're able to continue reading.

HOW TO USE THIS INSTRUCTIONAL STRATEGY

Students participate in grand conversations in small groups and together as a class. Teachers follow these steps in using this procedure:

1 **Read the book.** Students read a story or part of story, or they listen to the teacher read it aloud.

2 **Prepare for the grand conversation.** Students think about the story by drawing pictures or writing in reading logs (see p. 113). This step is especially important when students don't talk much because with this preparation, they're more likely to have ideas to share with classmates.

3 **Have small-group conversations.** Students form small groups to talk about the story before getting together as a class. This step is optional and is generally used when students are uncomfortable about sharing with the whole class or when they need more time to talk about the story.

4 **Begin the grand conversation.** Students form a circle for the class conversation so that everyone can see each other. Teachers begin by asking, "Who would like to begin?" or "What are you thinking about?" One student makes a comment, and classmates take turns talking about the idea the first student introduced.

5 **Continue the conversation.** A student introduces a new idea, and classmates talk about it, sharing ideas, asking questions, making connections, and reading excerpts from the story to make a point. Students limit their comments to the idea being discussed, and after students finish discussing this idea, a new one is introduced. To ensure that everyone participates, teachers often ask students to make no more than three comments until everyone has spoken at least once.

6 **Ask questions.** Teachers ask questions to direct students to aspects of the story that have been missed; for example, they might focus on an element of story structure or the author's craft. Or they may ask students to compare the book to the film version of the story or to other books by the same author.

7 Conclude the conversation. After all of the big ideas have been explored, teachers end the conversation by summarizing and drawing conclusions about the story or the chapter of the novel.

8 Reflect on the conversation. Students write (or write again) in reading logs to reflect on the ideas discussed in the grand conversation.

WHEN TO USE THIS INSTRUCTIONAL STRATEGY

Students participate in grand conversations when they're reading novels and picture-book stories during literature focus units and literature circles. When students meet for a whole-class conversation, a feeling of community is established. Young children usually meet as a class, and older students get together as a class when they're participating in a literature focus unit or listening to the teacher read a book aloud to the class. But during literature circles, students meet in small groups because they're reading different books, and they want to have more opportunities to talk. When the entire class meets, students have only a few opportunities to talk, but when they meet in small groups, they have many more opportunities to share their ideas.

REFERENCES

Bunting, E. (1999). *Smoky night*. New York: Voyager.

Coville, B. (2002). *Jeremy Thatcher, dragon hatcher*. New York: Aladdin Books.

DiCamillo, K. (2006). *The tale of Despereaux*. Cambridge; MA: Candlewick Press.

Fleischman, P. (2004). *Seedfolks*. New York: Harper Trophy.

Graves, M. F., & Fitzgerald, J. (2003). Scaffolding reading experiences for multilingual classrooms. In G. G. Garcia (Ed.), *English learners: Reaching the highest level of English literacy* (pp. 96–124). Newark, DE: International Reading Association.

Hale, S. (2007). *Princess Academy*. Bloomsbury.

Henkes, K. (1996). *Chrysanthemum*. New York: Harper Trophy.

Martinez, M. G., & Roser, N. L. (1995). The books make a difference in story talk. In N. L. Roser & M. G. Martinez (Eds.). *Book talk and beyond: Children and teachers respond to literature* (pp. 32–41). Newark, DE: International Reading Association.

Peterson, R., & Eeds, M. (2007). *Grand conversations: Literature groups in action* (Updated ed.). New York: Scholastic.

Wiesner, D. (2006). *Flotsam*. New York: Clarion Books.

17 Guided Reading

Instructional Focus		Grade Levels
☐ Oral Language	☑ Comprehension	☑ PreK–Grade 2
☑ Phonemic Awareness/Phonics	☐ Writing	☐ Grades 3–5
☑ Fluency	☐ Spelling	☐ Grades 6–8
☐ Vocabulary	☐ Content Areas	☑ English Learners

Guided reading is a small-group instructional strategy that teachers use to read a book with a small group of students who read at approximately the same instructional level (Clay, 1991). Teachers select a book that students can read at their instructional level, that is, with approximately 90% accuracy, and they support students' reading and their use of strategies during guided reading (Depree & Iversen, 1996; Fountas & Pinnell, 1996). Students do the actual reading themselves, and they usually read silently at their own pace through the entire book. Emergent readers often mumble the words softly as they read, and this helps the teacher keep track of students' reading and the strategies they're using. Guided reading isn't round-robin reading, in which students take turns reading pages aloud to the group.

WHY USE THIS INSTRUCTIONAL STRATEGY

The goal of guided reading is for students to become fluent, capable readers. Students read books that are appropriate for their reading level, and they have their teachers sitting with them to teach strategies and skills and to provide guidance when necessary.

Scaffolding English Learners

Teachers use guided reading with young English learners just as they do with their English-speaking classmates. This instructional strategy can also be used with older English learners who are struggling readers, especially if they aren't fluent and don't know how to use word-identification and comprehension strategies. It's important to choose the right books for older students—ones that are appropriate for both their interests and their reading levels. Peregoy and Boyle (2009) point out that guided reading is effective with English learners because they can experience success as they read interesting books in small, comfortable groups with teacher support and guidance.

COMMON CORE STATE STANDARDS FOR ENGLISH LANGUAGE ARTS: *GUIDED READING*

This instructional strategy supports these Common Core State Standards for Reading: Foundational Skills:

- Students apply grade-level phonics and word-analysis skills to decode words.
- Students read with sufficient fluency to support comprehension.
- Students use context to self-correct errors.

Students also learn about the features of fiction and nonfiction texts through guided reading lessons.

HOW TO USE THIS INSTRUCTIONAL STRATEGY

Teachers organize students into small, flexible groups for guided reading according to their reading level, and they make changes to meet students' changing needs. The steps in the instructional strategy vary according to students' needs and their reading levels, but they generally include these steps:

1 Choose an appropriate book. Teachers choose a book that students in the small group can read with 90% accuracy. They collect a copy of the book for each student.

2 Introduce the book. Teachers set the purpose for reading and show the book's cover, reading the title and the author's name. Next, they activate students' background knowledge on a topic related to the book, often introducing key vocabulary as they talk, but they don't use vocabulary flash cards to drill students on new words. Students "picture walk" through the book, looking at the illustrations, talking about them, and making predictions. And finally, teachers briefly mention some of the strategies that good readers use that they've already taught to these students and remind them to use them as they read.

3 Read the book. Teachers provide support with decoding and reading strategies as needed while students read. Depending on their reading level, students either "mumble-read" softly or read silently. Teachers observe students as they read and assess their use of word-identification and comprehension strategies. They help individual students decode unfamiliar words, deal with unfamiliar sentence structures, and comprehend ideas presented in the text whenever assistance is required. They offer prompts, such as "Look at how that word ends" or "Does that make sense?"

4 Encourage students to respond. Students talk about the book, ask questions, and relate it to others they've read, as in a grand conversation (see p. 45). Teachers also compliment students on the strategies they used while they were reading.

5 Revisit the text. Teachers use the text that students have just read to demonstrate a comprehension strategy, teach a phonics concept or word-identification skill, or review new vocabulary words.

6 Provide opportunities for independent reading. Teachers place the book in a book basket or in the classroom library so that students can reread it.

WHEN TO USE THIS INSTRUCTIONAL STRATEGY

Teachers teach guided reading lessons to small groups of students using leveled books while their classmates are involved in other literacy activities (Cunningham, Hall, & Sigmon, 2000). Classmates are often reading independently, writing books, and doing phonics and spelling activities at centers. Teachers rotate the groups every 20–30 minutes so that students participate in a variety of teacher-directed and independent activities each day. To learn more about guided reading, check the Booklist on page 50; it contains books for teachers on using guided reading and leveled books with primary grade students as well as students in fourth through sixth grades.

BOOKLIST

Guided Reading

Boushey, G., & Moser, J. (2006). *The daily five.* Portland, ME: Stenhouse.

Burke, T., & Hartzold, K. (2007). *Guided reading: One lesson, all levels, any text.* Peterborough, NH: Crystal Springs Books.

Fountas, I. C., & Pinnell, G. S. (1996). *Guided reading: Good first teaching for all children.* Portsmouth, NH: Heinemann.

Fountas, I. C., & Pinnell, G. S. (2001). *Guiding readers and writers grades 3–6: Teaching comprehension, genre, and content literacy.* Portsmouth, NH: Heinemann.

Pinnell, G. S., & Fountas, I C. (1999). *Matching books to readers: Using leveled books in guided reading, K–3.* Portsmouth, NH: Heinemann.

Richardson, J. (2009). *The next step in guided reading: Focused assessment and targeted lessons for helping every student become a better reader.* New York: Scholastic.

Saunders-Smith, G. S. (2009). *The ultimate guided reading how-to book* (2nd ed.). Thousand Oaks, CA: Corwin.

Schulman, M. B. (2006). *Guided reading in grades 3–6.* New York: Scholastic.

Tyner, B. (2009). *Small-group reading instruction: A differentiated model for beginning and struggling readers.* Newark, DE: International Reading Association.

Witherell, N. L. (2007). *The guided reading classroom: How to keep all students working constructively.* Portsmouth, NH: Heinemann.

REFERENCES

Clay, M. M. (1991). *Becoming literate: The construction of inner control.* Portsmouth, NH: Heinemann.

Cunningham, P. M., Hall, D. P., & Sigmon, C. M. (2000). *The teacher's guide to the four blocks: A multimethod, multilevel framework for grades 1–3.* Greensboro, NC: Carson-Dellosa.

Depree, H., & Iversen, S. (1996). *Early literacy in the classroom: A new standard for young readers.* Bothell, WA: Wright Group.

Fountas, I. C., & Pinnell, G. S. (1996). *Guided reading: Good first teaching for all children.* Portsmouth, NH: Heinemann.

Peregoy, S. F., & Boyle, O. F. (2009). *Reading, writing, and learning in ESL: A resource book for K–12 teachers* (5th ed.). Boston: Allyn & Bacon.

18 Hot Seat

Instructional Focus

☑ Oral Language	☑ Comprehension
☐ Phonemic Awareness/Phonics	☐ Writing
☐ Fluency	☐ Spelling
☐ Vocabulary	☑ Content Areas

Grade Levels

☐ PreK–Grade 2
☑ Grades 3–5
☑ Grades 6–8
☐ English Learners

Hot seat is a role-playing activity that builds students' comprehension. Students assume the persona of a character in a story, the featured person in a biography, an author whose books they've read, or a well-known real-life figure and sit in a chair designated as the "hot seat" to be interviewed by classmates. It's called *hot seat* because students have to think quickly and respond to their classmates' questions and comments. Wilhelm (2002) explains that through the hot seat activity, students get to explore the characters, analyze story events and draw inferences, and try out different interpretations. Students aren't intimidated by the activity; in fact, in most classrooms, it's very popular. Students are usually eager for their turn to sit in the hot seat. They often wear a costume they've created when they assume a character's persona and share information about the character with classmates. They also collect objects and make artifacts to share.

WHY USE THIS INSTRUCTIONAL STRATEGY

As students participate in the activity, they deepen their understanding of what they're reading. This instructional strategy develops students' ability to think on their feet as they analyze characters and draw inferences. Students also have opportunities to refine their oral language abilities as they give presentations, ask questions, and interview classmates.

HOW TO USE THIS INSTRUCTIONAL STRATEGY

Hot seat is usually a whole-class activity, but when students are participating in literature circles, each small group can conduct its own hot seat activity. Here are the steps in the procedure:

1 **Learn about the character.** Students prepare for the hot seat activity by reading a story or a biography to learn about the character they'll impersonate.

COMMON CORE STATE STANDARDS FOR ENGLISH LANGUAGE ARTS: *HOT SEAT*

This instructional strategy supports these Common Core State Standards for Speaking and Listening:

- Students present information clearly and coherently.
- Students keep appropriate eye contact with the audience.
- Students integrate visual or multimedia displays into their presentations.

Students use information they've learned from reading literature or nonfiction books for their oral presentations.

2 **Create a costume.** Students design a costume appropriate for their character. In addition, they often collect objects or create artifacts to use in their presentations.

3 **Prepare opening remarks.** Students think about the most important things they'd like to share about the character and plan what they'll say at the beginning of the activity.

4 **Introduce the character.** One student sits in front of classmates in a chair designated as the "hot seat," tells a little about the character he or she is role-playing using a first-person viewpoint (e.g., "I said 'One small step for man, one giant leap for mankind'"), and shares artifacts.

5 **Ask questions and make comments.** Classmates ask thoughtful questions to learn more about the character and offer advice, and the student remains in the role to respond to them.

6 **Summarize the ideas.** The student in the hot seat selects a classmate to summarize the important ideas that were presented about the character. He or she clarifies any misunderstandings and adds any big ideas that classmates didn't mention.

WHEN TO USE THIS INSTRUCTIONAL STRATEGY

When students are reading a story during a literature focus unit, they can take turns role-playing different characters from the story and sitting in the hot seat to be interviewed. Students representing different characters can also come together for a conversation—a group hot seat activity. For example, during a literature focus unit on *The View From Saturday* (Konigsburg, 1998), the story of a championship sixth grade Academic Bowl team that's told from the perspectives of the team members, students representing the team— Noah, Nadia, Ethan, and Julian—and their teacher, Mrs. Olinski, can take turns sitting in the hot seat, or they can come together to talk about the story. For a list of additional stories told from multiple viewpoints, check the Booklist below. Similarly, when students are participating in literature circles, they can take turns role-playing different characters from the story they're reading, or each student in the group can assume the persona of a different character at the same time for a group hot seat activity. After students read biographies, they sit in the hot seat to share what they've learned with their classmates.

BOOKLIST

Stories Told From Multiple Viewpoints

Fleischman, P. (2004). *Seedfolks.* New York: Harper Trophy. M

Hesse, K. (2005). *Witness.* New York: Scholastic. U

Konigsburg, E. L. (1998). *The view from Saturday.* New York: Atheneum. U

Lester, J. (2000). *To be a slave.* New York: Puffin Books. U

Lester, J. (2007). *Day of tears.* New York: Hyperion Books. U

Peet, M. (2008). *Tamar.* Cambridge, MA: Candlewick Press. U

Schlitz, L. A. (2007). *Good masters! Sweet ladies! Voices from a medieval village.* Cambridge, MA: Candlewick Press. U

Stier, C. (2011). *The terrible secrets of the tell-all club.* New York: Whitman. MU

Williams-Garcia, R. (2010). *One crazy summer.* New York: Amistad. U

Yang, G. L. (2008). *American born Chinese.* New York: Square Fish Books. U

M = middle grades (3–5); U = upper grades (6–8)

REFERENCES

Konigsburg, E. L. (1998). *The view from Saturday.* New York: Atheneum.

Wilhelm, J. D. (2002). *Action strategies for deepening comprehension.* New York: Scholastic.

19 Interactive Read-Alouds

Instructional Focus		Grade Levels
☑ Oral Language	☑ Comprehension	☑ PreK–Grade 2
☐ Phonemic Awareness/Phonics	☐ Writing	☑ Grades 3–5
☐ Fluency	☐ Spelling	☑ Grades 6–8
☐ Vocabulary	☑ Content Areas	☑ English Learners

Interactive read-alouds are the best way for teachers to share books with students. The focus is on comprehension, and interpretation is enhanced because students are engaged in the reading process before, during, and after reading. Teachers introduce the book and activate students' background knowledge before they begin to read. Next, they engage students while they read aloud through brief discussions and other activities. Then after reading, they provide opportunities for students to respond to the book. What's most important is how teachers engage students while they're reading aloud (Fisher, Flood, Lapp, & Frey, 2004).

One way teachers engage students is to stop reading periodically to discuss what has just been read. The timing is crucial: If they're reading stories, it's more effective to stop at points where students can make predictions and connections, after reading episodes that students might find confusing, and just before it becomes clear how the story will end. If they're reading nonfiction books, teachers stop to talk about big ideas as they're presented, briefly explain technical terms, and emphasize connections among the big ideas. If they're reading poems, teachers often read the entire poem once, and then stop as they read it a second time for students to play with words, notice poetic devices, and repeat favorite words and lines. The box on page 54 lists interactive techniques for each genre. Deciding how often to stop for discussion or another activity and when to continue reading develops through practice and varies from one group of students to another.

WHY USE THIS INSTRUCTIONAL STRATEGY

Reading aloud is a cherished classroom routine, and the interactive read-aloud procedure is an effective instructional strategy. Researchers have concluded that students are better listeners when they're involved during the reading, not afterward (Dickinson & Tabors, 2001). This conclusion led to the development of the interactive read-aloud procedure (Barrentine, 1996).

COMMON CORE STATE STANDARDS FOR ENGLISH LANGUAGE ARTS: *INTERACTIVE READ-ALOUDS*

This instructional strategy supports these Common Core State Standards for Reading: Literature, Reading: Informational Text, and Speaking and Listening:

- Students listen to and comprehend grade-appropriate literature and informational texts.
- Students ask and answer questions about texts being read aloud.
- Students interpret information being read aloud.

Students demonstrate engagement and comprehension during interactive read-alouds.

Scaffolding English Learners

Listening to the teacher read aloud places heavy cognitive and linguistic demands on English learners, so teachers often read aloud the book or section of the book twice (Peregoy & Boyle, 2009). During the first reading, teachers engage students by asking them to make predictions, and they also stop to discuss an illustration or to summarize what's been read. Then during the second reading, teachers stop to encourage students to talk about the book.

Interactive read-alouds are especially important for English learners for several reasons: They provide an opportunity for students to listen to age-appropriate texts that they couldn't read on their own, they build essential background knowledge on a topic along with new vocabulary words, and the students learn about literary genres and structures (Rothenberg & Fisher, 2007).

HOW TO USE THIS INSTRUCTIONAL STRATEGY

This whole-class activity is easy to implement, as long as teachers have planned how they'll engage students with the text. They follow these steps as they use this procedure:

1 **Pick a book.** Teachers choose award-winning and other high-quality books that are appropriate for students and that fit into their instructional programs.

2 **Preview the book.** Teachers practice reading the book to ensure that they can read it fluently and to decide where to pause and engage students with the text; they write prompts on self-stick notes to mark these pages. Teachers also think about how they'll introduce the book and select difficult vocabulary words to highlight.

3 **Introduce the book.** Teachers activate students' background knowledge, set a clear purpose for listening, and preview the text.

Interactive Techniques	
Stories	• Make and revise predictions at pivotal points in the story.
	• Share personal, world, literary, and media connections.
	• Talk about what students are visualizing or how they're using other strategies.
	• Draw a picture of a character or an event.
	• Assume the persona of a character and share what the character might be thinking.
	• Reenact a scene from the story.
Nonfiction	• Ask questions or share information.
	• Raise hands when specific information is read.
	• Restate the headings as questions.
	• Take notes.
	• Complete graphic organizers.
Poetry	• Add sound effects.
	• Mumble-read along with the teacher.
	• Repeat lines after the teacher.
	• Clap when rhyming words, alliteration, onomatopoeia, or other poetic devices are heard.
	• Do a choral reading.

4 **Read the book interactively.** Teachers read the book aloud, modeling fluent and expressive reading. They stop periodically to ask questions to focus students on specific points in the text and involve them in other activities.

5 **Involve students in after-reading activities.** Students participate in discussions and other types of response activities.

WHEN TO USE THIS INSTRUCTIONAL STRATEGY

Teachers use this instructional strategy whenever they're reading aloud, no matter whether it's an after-lunch read-aloud period or during a literature focus unit, reading workshop, or a thematic unit. Reading aloud has always been a cherished time in kindergarten and first grade classrooms. Sometimes teachers think they should read to children only until they learn to read for themselves, but reading aloud to share the excitement of books, especially those that students can't read themselves, should remain an important part of the curriculum at all grade levels (Hahn, 2002). Upper grade students report that when they listen to the teacher read aloud, they get more interested in the book and understand it better, and the experience often makes them want to read it themselves (Ivey, 2003). In addition, Albright (2002) examined her seventh graders' responses during interactive read-alouds of picture books and found that through the activity, they were more engaged in learning, they exhibited high-level thinking, and they enriched their content-area knowledge.

REFERENCES

Albright, L. K. (2002). Bringing the Ice Maiden to life: Engaging adolescents in learning through picture book read-alouds in content areas. *Journal of Adolescent & Adult Literacy, 45,* 418–428.

Barrentine, S. J. (1996). Engaging with reading through interactive read-alouds. *The Reading Teacher, 50,* 36–43.

Dickinson, D. K., & Tabors, P. O. (2001). *Beginning literacy with language.* Baltimore: Brookes.

Fisher, D., Flood, K., Lapp, D., & Frey, N. (2004). Interactive read-alouds: Is there a common set of implementation practices? *The Reading Teacher, 58,* 8–17.

Hahn, M. L. (2002). *Reconsidering read-aloud.* Portland, ME: Stenhouse.

Ivey, G. (2003). "The teacher makes it more explainable" and other reasons to read aloud in the intermediate grades. *The Reading Teacher, 56,* 812–814.

Peregoy, S. F., & Boyle, O. F. (2009). *Reading, writing and learning in ESL: A resource book for K–12 teachers* (5th ed.). Boston: Allyn & Bacon.

Rothenberg, C., & Fisher, D. (2007). *Teaching English language learners: A differentiated approach.* Upper Saddle River, NJ: Merrill/Pearson.

20 Interactive Writing

Instructional Focus

- ☐ Oral Language
- ☑ Phonemic Awareness/Phonics
- ☑ Fluency
- ☐ Vocabulary
- ☐ Comprehension
- ☑ Writing
- ☑ Spelling
- ☑ Content Areas

Grade Levels

- ☑ PreK–Grade 2
- ☐ Grades 3–5
- ☐ Grades 6–8
- ☑ English Learners

In interactive writing, students and the teacher create a text and "share the pen" as they write the text on chart paper (Button, Johnson, & Furgerson, 1996). The text is composed by the group, and the teacher guides students as they write the text word by word on chart paper. Students take turns writing known letters and familiar words, adding punctuation marks, and marking spaces between words. All students participate in creating and writing the text on chart paper, and they also write the text on small whiteboards. After writing, students read and reread the text using shared reading (see p. 123).

WHY USE THIS INSTRUCTIONAL STRATEGY

Interactive writing is used to show students how writing works and how to construct words using their knowledge of sound–symbol correspondences and spelling patterns (Tompkins & Collom, 2004). This instructional strategy was developed by the well-known British educator Moira McKenzie, who based it on Don Holdaway's work in shared reading (Fountas & Pinnell, 1996).

Scaffolding English Learners

Interactive writing is a powerful instructional procedure to use with English learners, no matter whether they're first graders or eighth graders. Teachers use the same procedure for English learners that they use with young children: They help the students negotiate a sentence and write it in Standard English. As they work with students, teachers take advantage of opportunities to reinforce English pronunciation, spelling rules, sentence structure, and conventions of print.

COMMON CORE STATE STANDARDS FOR ENGLISH LANGUAGE ARTS: *INTERACTIVE WRITING*

This instructional strategy supports these Common Core State Standards for Reading: Foundational Skills, Writing, and Language:

- Students write informative texts and opinion pieces with guidance from teachers.
- Students apply grade-level phonics and word-analysis skills.
- Students use Standard English spelling and other conventions.

Students apply their knowledge about written language during interactive writing projects.

HOW TO USE THIS INSTRUCTIONAL STRATEGY

Teachers usually do interactive writing with small groups of students or the entire class, depending on students' developmental levels and their instructional needs. They follow this procedure:

1. **Collect materials for interactive writing.** Teachers collect chart paper, colored marking pens, white correction tape, an alphabet chart, magnetic letters or letter cards, and a pointer. They also collect these materials for individual students' writing: small whiteboards, pens, and erasers.

2. **Set a purpose.** Teachers present a stimulus activity or set a purpose for the interactive writing activity. Often they read or reread a trade book as a stimulus, but students also can write daily news, compose a letter, or brainstorm information they're learning in social studies or science.

3. **Choose a sentence to write.** Teachers negotiate the text—often a sentence or two—with students. Students think of a sentence and repeat it several times, and then they segment it into words. The teacher also helps the students remember the sentence as it's written.

4. **Pass out writing supplies.** Teachers distribute individual whiteboards, pens, and erasers for students to use to write the text individually as it is written together as a class on chart paper. They periodically ask students to hold their boards up to show what they're writing.

5. **Write the first sentence.** Before writing the first word, the teacher and students slowly pronounce the word, "pulling" it from their mouths or "stretching" it out. Then students take turns writing the letters in the first word. The teacher chooses students to write each sound or the entire word, depending on their knowledge of phonics and spelling. Teachers often have students write with one color pen, and they use another color to write the parts of words that students can't spell; in this way, teachers keep track of how much writing students are able to do. Teachers keep a poster with the upper- and lowercase letters of the alphabet available for students to refer to when they don't know how to form a letter, and they use white correction tape (sometimes called "boo-boo" tape) when students form a letter incorrectly or write the wrong letter. After writing each word, one student serves as the "spacer" and uses his or her hand to mark the spaces between words and sentences. Students reread the sentence from the beginning each time a new word is completed. When appropriate, teachers call attention to capital letters, punctuation marks, and other conventions of print. They repeat this procedure to write additional sentences to complete the text.

6. **Display the interactive writing.** After the writing is completed, teachers post the chart in the classroom and have students reread the text using shared or independent reading. Students often reread interactive charts when they "read the room." They may also add artwork to "finish" the chart.

WHEN TO USE THIS INSTRUCTIONAL STRATEGY

Interactive writing can be used during literature focus units, in social studies and science thematic units, and for many other purposes (Keogh, 2005). Here are some applications:

Write predictions before reading

Write responses after reading

Write letters and other messages

Make lists

Write daily news

Rewrite a familiar story

Write information or facts

Write recipes

Make K-W-L charts (see p. 60), clusters (see p. 21), data charts (see p. 31), and other diagrams

Create innovations, or new versions of a familiar text

Write class poems

Write words on a word wall (see p. 156)

Make posters

When children begin interactive writing in kindergarten, they write letters to represent the beginning sounds in words and write familiar words, such as *the, a,* and *is.* The first letters that children write are often the letters in their own names, particularly the first letter. As they learn more about sound–symbol correspondences and spelling patterns, they do more of the writing. Once students are writing words fluently, they can continue to do interactive writing as they work in small groups. Each student in the group uses a particular color pen and takes turns writing letters, letter clusters, and words. They also get accustomed to using the white correction tape to correct poorly formed letters and misspelled words. Students also sign their names in color on the page so that the teacher can track which student wrote which words. A black-and-white copy of a small group's interactive writing about snails is shown on the next page. The boxes around two letters and one word represent the white correction tape that students used.

Differentiating Instruction

Teachers use the interactive writing strategy to individualize instruction and meet students' needs using these adaptations:

- Teachers work with small groups of prekindergartners who are interested in writing longer messages.
- Teachers use interactive writing with older students who are struggling writers.
- Teachers have students reread interactive writing charts to practice reading high-frequency words.
- Teachers ask students to look for words representing a phonics pattern during minilessons.
- Teachers have students search for examples of capitalization and punctuation during minilessons.

Through these adaptations, students learn more about written language and gain confidence in themselves as writers.

A Small Group's Interactive Writing

SnaiL

The SMaiL eats CUcum
Bers,
He cLimBS oN the WaLL.
Mai   kimberly
NaLee ChriS
Cindy Mrs. F.

REFERENCES

Button, K., Johnson, M. J., & Furgerson, P. (1996). Interactive writing in a primary classroom. *The Reading Teacher*, 49, 446–454.

Fountas, I. C., & Pinnell, G. S. (1996). *Guided reading: Good first teaching for all children*. Portsmouth, NH: Heinemann.

Keogh, V. K. (2005). Interactive writing: Teaching skills in context. In G. E. Tompkins & C. Blanchfield (Eds.), *50 ways to develop strategic writers* (pp. 64–66). Upper Saddle River, NJ: Merrill/Prentice Hall.

Tompkins, G. E., & Collom, S. (Eds.). (2004). *Sharing the pen: Interactive writing with young children*. Upper Saddle River, NJ: Merrill/Prentice Hall.

21 K-W-L Charts

Instructional Focus		Grade Levels
☐ Oral Language	☑ Comprehension	☑ PreK–Grade 2
☐ Phonemic Awareness/Phonics	☐ Writing	☑ Grades 3–5
☐ Fluency	☐ Spelling	☑ Grades 6–8
☑ Vocabulary	☑ Content Areas	☑ English Learners

Teachers use K-W-L charts to activate students' background knowledge about a topic and to scaffold them as they ask questions and organize the information they're learning (Ogle, 1986, 1989). Teachers create a K-W-L chart by hanging up three sheets of butcher paper on a classroom wall and labeling them *K*, *W*, and *L*; the letters stand for "What We **K**now," "What We **W**onder" or "What We **W**ant to Learn," and "What We **L**earned." A K-W-L chart that a kindergarten class developed as they were hatching chicks is shown on the next page. The teacher did the actual writing on the chart, but the children generated the ideas and the questions.

This instructional strategy takes several weeks or longer to complete because it spans a thematic unit. Teachers introduce a K-W-L chart at the beginning of the unit and use it to identify what students already know about the topic and what they want to learn. Then at the end of the unit, students complete the last section of the chart, documenting what they've learned.

WHY USE THIS INSTRUCTIONAL STRATEGY

This instructional procedure helps students combine new information with background knowledge and develop technical vocabulary related to a thematic unit. As they create a K-W-L chart, students become curious and more engaged in the learning process, and teachers have opportunities to introduce complex ideas and technical vocabulary in a nonthreatening way. Teachers direct, scribe, and monitor the development of the K-W-L chart, but it's the students' talk that makes this such a powerful instructional strategy. Students use talk to explore ideas as they complete the K and W columns and to share new knowledge as they finish the L column.

COMMON CORE STATE STANDARDS FOR ENGLISH LANGUAGE ARTS: *K-W-L CHARTS*

This instructional strategy supports these Common Core State Standards for Reading: Informational Text and Writing:

- Students recall information from print and digital sources.
- Students identify main ideas and related details.
- Students determine relationships among main ideas.

Students use K-W-L charts to gather and organize ideas as they investigate nonfiction topics.

A Kindergarten Class's K-W-L Chart		
K What We **Know**	**W** What We **Want** to Learn	**L** What We **Learned**
They hatch from eggs. They sleep. They can be yellow or other colors. They have 2 legs. They have 2 wings. They eat food. They have a tail. They live on a farm. They are little. They have beaks. They are covered with fluff.	Are their feet called wabbly? Do they live in the woods? What are their bodies covered with? How many toes do they have? Do they have a stomach? What noises do they make? Do they like the sun?	Chickens' bodies are covered with feathers. Chickens have 4 claws. Yes, they do have stomachs. Chickens like to play in the sun. They like to stay warm. They live on farms.

Scaffolding English Learners

Teachers often use K-W-L charts with English learners because this instructional strategy exemplifies many of the characteristics of effective instruction for students who are learning English: Students participate in collaborative groups to develop their background knowledge and vocabulary about a broad topic (Peregoy & Boyle, 2009). Teachers often use pictures to support students' learning. Sometimes students look through picture books related to the topic as they complete the K column of the chart and at other times, they draw small illustrations of the information that they add to the chart.

HOW TO USE THIS INSTRUCTIONAL STRATEGY

Younger children work together to make class charts; older students make K-W-L charts in pairs or small groups, or they make individual charts to organize and document their learning. Teachers follow these steps to make class K-W-L charts:

1 **Post a K-W-L chart.** Teachers post a large chart on the classroom wall, divide it into three columns, and label them *K* (What We **K**now), *W* (What We **W**onder or What We **W**ant to Learn), and *L* (What We **L**earned).

2 **Complete the K column.** At the beginning of a thematic unit, teachers ask students to brainstorm what they know about the topic and write this information in the K column. Sometimes students suggest information that isn't correct; these statements should be turned into questions and added to the W column.

3 **Complete the W column.** Teachers write the questions that students suggest in the W column. They continue to add questions during the unit.

4 **Complete the L column.** At the end of the unit, students reflect on what they've learned, and teachers record this information in the L column of the chart.

WHEN TO USE THIS INSTRUCTIONAL STRATEGY

K-W-L charts support students' learning of nonfiction topics during thematic units. Even though each of the three columns on a K-W-L chart plays an important role in learning, sometimes teachers adapt the K-W-L format and use only two columns, either the K and L columns or the W and L columns, depending on available time and instructional needs. When teachers use only the W and L columns, for example, they have students brainstorm questions after previewing a chapter in a social studies textbook and then add what they learn in the L column to complete the chart after reading the chapter.

A Fourth Grader's Flip Chart

S   8 legs
P   make webs
I   catch insects
D   eat them
E   Black Widow
R   Tarantula
S   bite
     some are
     poisonous

Differentiating Instruction

Teachers use K-W-L charts to help students activate background knowledge and gather information about nonfiction topics using these adaptations:

- English learners examine artifacts, photos, and picture books when developing the K and W sections of the chart, and then they draw diagrams and illustrations to share their learning for the L section.

- Students create individual flip book K-W-L charts, made by folding a legal-size sheet of paper in half, lengthwise, cutting the top flap into thirds, labeling the flaps *K*, *W*, and *L*, and writing information in each column, as shown on the previous page.

- Students organize the information on the K-W-L chart into categories to highlight the big ideas; this strategy is called K-W-L Plus (Carr & Ogle, 1987).

- When students are using K-W-L charts as a research tool, they add a fourth column, "H—How Do We Find Information?" between the W and L columns and list appropriate resources—websites, reference books, experts to interview, for instance—for answering questions in the W column.

- Students demonstrate their learning during a thematic unit by creating their own L columns and explaining what they've learned using a combination of sentences, diagrams, and illustrations.

Through these adaptations, teachers teach research strategies and support students' learning of content-area topics.

REFERENCES

Carr, E., & Ogle, D. (1987). K-W-L Plus: A strategy for comprehension and summarization. *Journal of Reading, 31*, 626–631.

Ogle, D. M. (1986). K-W-L: A teaching model that develops active reading of expository text. *The Reading Teacher, 39*, 564–570.

Ogle, D. M. (1989). The know, want to know, learn strategy. In K. D. Muth (Ed.), *Children's comprehension of text: Research into practice* (pp. 205–223). Newark, DE: International Reading Association.

Peregoy, S. F., & Boyle, O. F. (2009). *Reading, writing, and learning in ESL: A resource book for K–12 teachers* (5th ed.). Boston: Allyn & Bacon.

22 Language Experience Approach

Instructional Focus		Grade Levels
☑ Oral Language	☐ Comprehension	☑ PreK–Grade 2
☐ Phonemic Awareness/Phonics	☑ Writing	☐ Grades 3–5
☑ Fluency	☐ Spelling	☐ Grades 6–8
☐ Vocabulary	☐ Content Areas	☑ English Learners

The Language Experience Approach (LEA) is based on children's language and experiences (Ashton-Warner, 1965; Stauffer, 1970). A child dictates words and sentences about an experience, and the teacher writes the dictation; as the words and sentences are written, the teacher models how written language works. The text that's written then becomes the child's reading material. Because the language comes from the child and because the content is based on his or her experiences, the child is usually able to read the text easily.

WHY USE THIS INSTRUCTIONAL STRATEGY

The Language Experience Approach is an effective way to help children emerge into reading because oral language is linked to written language. Even children who haven't been successful with other types of reading activities can read what they've dictated (Shanker & Cockrum, 2008). There is a drawback, however: Teachers provide a "perfect" model when they take children's dictation—they write neatly and spell words correctly. After LEA activities, some young children are reluctant to do their own writing; they prefer their teacher's "perfect" writing to their own childlike writing. To avoid this problem, young children should be doing their own writing in journals and books and participating in interactive writing activities (see p. 56) at the same time they're participating in Language Experience activities so they'll learn that sometimes they do their own writing and at other times, the teacher takes their dictation.

Scaffolding English Learners

Teachers use the Language Experience Approach to create reading materials that English learners can read and that interest them. Students cut pictures out of magazines and glue them in a book. Then the teacher and students identify and label several important words in a picture and create a sentence related to it. Then the teacher writes the sentence underneath the picture and the students reread it. LEA is an effective instructional strategy because students are creating and reading texts that are relevant to them (Crawford, 2003; Landis, Umolu, & Mancha, 2010).

COMMON CORE STATE STANDARDS FOR ENGLISH LANGUAGE ARTS: *LANGUAGE EXPERIENCE APPROACH*

This instructional strategy supports these Common Core State Standards for Reading: Foundational Skills:

- Students demonstrate their understanding of print concepts as they dictate and read texts.
- Students apply phonics and word-analysis skills when they read their dictated texts.
- Students read and reread texts with fluency and understanding.

Students develop concepts about written language when they create Language Experience stories.

HOW TO USE THIS INSTRUCTIONAL STRATEGY

This flexible strategy can be used with the entire class, with small groups, and with individual students, depending on the teacher's purpose. Teachers follow this procedure:

1. **Provide an experience.** The experience serves as the stimulus for the writing; it can be an experience shared in school, a book read aloud, a field trip, or some other experience that students are familiar with, such as having a pet or playing in the snow.

2. **Talk about the experience.** The teacher and students talk about the experience to review it so that the students' dictation will be more interesting and complete. Teachers often begin with an open-ended question, such as "What are we going to write about?" As students talk about their experiences, they clarify and organize ideas, use more specific vocabulary, and extend their understanding.

3. **Record the students' dictation.** Students suggest sentences to dictate, and with the teacher's guidance, the text takes shape. The teacher writes the sentences on chart paper, and after writing each sentence, the teacher rereads it. The teacher tries to write students' dictation verbatim but changes nonstandard usage to Standard English, especially if the chart will be posted in the classroom for all students to reread.

4. **Read the text aloud.** The teacher reads the text aloud, pointing at each word as it's read; this reading reminds students of the content of the text and demonstrates how to read it aloud with appropriate intonation. Then students read along with the teacher. After several joint readings, most students can read the text independently or with a buddy.

5. **Extend the reading experience.** Students often reread the chart together as a class, in small groups, and individually. The teacher often puts a sheet of plastic over the chart so students can circle high-frequency words or words illustrating phonics concepts or spelling patterns. They also pick out capital letters and punctuation marks or other concepts about written language they're learning.

6. **Make sentence strips.** Teachers rewrite the text on sentence strips that students keep in a pocket attached to the back of the chart. The students read and sequence the sentence strips, and after they can read the sentence strips smoothly, they cut the strips into individual words. Students arrange the words into the familiar sentence and then create new sentences with the word cards.

WHEN TO USE THIS INSTRUCTIONAL STRATEGY

The Language Experience Approach is often used to create texts students can read and use as a resource for writing in thematic units. For example, during a science unit on ladybugs in a first and second grade combination class, the teacher read aloud stories and nonfiction books about these fascinating insects, and with this knowledge, children dictated this text:

Part 1: What Ladybugs Do

Ladybugs are helper insects. They help people because they eat aphids. They make the earth pretty. They are red and they have 7 black spots. Ladybugs keep their wings under the red wing cases. Their wings are transparent and they fly with these wings. Ladybugs love to eat aphids. They love them so much that they can eat 50 aphids in one day!

Part 2: How Ladybugs Grow

Ladybugs live on leaves in bushes and in tree trunks. They lay eggs that are sticky and yellow on a leaf. The eggs hatch and out come tiny and black larvae. They like to eat aphids, too. Next the larva becomes a pupa and then it changes into a ladybug. When the ladybugs first come out of the pupa, they are yellow but they change into red and their spots appear. Then they can fly.

Part 3: Ladybugs Are Smart

Ladybugs have a good trick so that the birds won't eat them. If a bird starts to attack, the ladybug turns over on her back and squeezes a stinky liquid from her legs. It smells terrible and makes the bird fly away.

Each part was written on a separate sheet of chart paper. Next, the children each chose a sentence to be written on a sentence strip. Some children wrote their own sentence, and the teacher wrote sentences for other children. They practiced reading their sentences and read them to classmates. Then they cut the sentences apart and rearranged them. Later, children used the sentences in class collaboration books (see p. 25) and individual "All About Ladybugs" books (turn to p. 1 to read about "All About . . ." books).

Teachers also use the Language Experience Approach with individual students who are struggling readers. Students dictate texts on topics of special interest to them that teachers record in notebooks, and then these texts become their reading materials. They participate in the same activities used with class charts: Students read and reread the texts, pick out high-frequency words and examples of written-language concepts in the text, and arrange sentence strips and word cards using the text. LEA is time-consuming, but it's an effective instructional strategy for both young beginning readers and older students who don't read fluently (Cowen, 2003).

REFERENCES

Ashton-Warner, S. (1965). *Teacher*. New York: Simon & Schuster.

Cowen, J. E. (2003). *A balanced approach to beginning reading instruction: A synthesis of six major U.S. research studies*. Newark, DE: International Reading Association.

Crawford, A. N. (2003). Communicative approaches to second-language acquisition: The bridge to second-language literacy. In G. G. Garcia (Ed.), *English learners: Reaching the highest level of English literacy* (pp. 152–181). Newark, DE: International Reading Association.

Landis, D., Umolu, J., & Mancha, S. (2010). The power of language experience for cross-cultural reading and writing. *The Reading Teacher, 63*, 580–589.

Shanker, J. L., & Cockrum, W. A. (2008). *Locating and correcting reading difficulties* (9th ed.). Boston: Allyn & Bacon/Pearson.

Stauffer, R. G. (1970). *Directing the reading-thinking process*. New York: Harper & Row.

23 Learning Logs

Instructional Focus

- ☐ Oral Language
- ☐ Phonemic Awareness/Phonics
- ☐ Fluency
- ☐ Vocabulary
- ☑ Comprehension
- ☑ Writing
- ☐ Spelling
- ☑ Content Areas

Grade Levels

- ☑ PreK–Grade 2
- ☑ Grades 3–5
- ☑ Grades 6–8
- ☐ English Learners

Students write in learning logs as part of thematic units. Learning logs, like other types of journals, are notebooks or booklets of paper in which students record information they're learning; they write questions, summaries, and reflections about their learning, and make charts and diagrams. Students' writing is impromptu in learning logs, and the emphasis is on using writing as a learning tool rather than on creating polished products. Even so, students should be encouraged to work carefully and to spell content-related words that have been posted on the word wall (see p. 156) correctly.

WHY USE THIS INSTRUCTIONAL STRATEGY

The great value of these journals is that students use them as tools for learning. As students write in learning logs, they explore new ideas, practice using new and technical vocabulary words, and personalize their learning (Strong, 2006). In addition, as teachers monitor students' logs, they can quickly check to see how well students understand the big ideas and what confusions they may have.

HOW TO USE THIS INSTRUCTIONAL STRATEGY

Students each construct learning logs at the beginning of a thematic unit, and then they make entries in the logs during the unit. Here is the procedure:

1 **Prepare learning logs.** At the beginning of a thematic unit, students construct learning logs using a combination of lined and unlined paper that's stapled into booklets with tagboard or laminated construction paper covers.

2 **Use learning logs.** Students take notes, draw diagrams, list vocabulary words, do quickwrites (see p. 99), and write summaries.

COMMON CORE STATE STANDARDS FOR ENGLISH LANGUAGE ARTS: *LEARNING LOGS*

This instructional strategy supports these Common Core State Standards for Reading: Informational Text and Writing:

- Students comprehend grade-appropriate informational texts.
- Students gather information from print and digital sources.
- Students identify key ideas and details, make connections among ideas, and analyze viewpoints.

Students build and integrate knowledge as they make entries in learning logs.

3 **Monitor students' entries.** Teachers read students' learning logs, answer their questions, and clarify confusions.

4 **Write reflections.** Teachers often have students review their entries at the end of the thematic unit and write a reflection about what they've learned.

WHEN TO USE THIS INSTRUCTIONAL STRATEGY

Students use learning logs during thematic units to make notes and respond to information they're learning as they read nonfiction books and chapters in content-area textbooks. They also make data charts (see p. 31), clusters (see p. 21), maps, time lines, and other

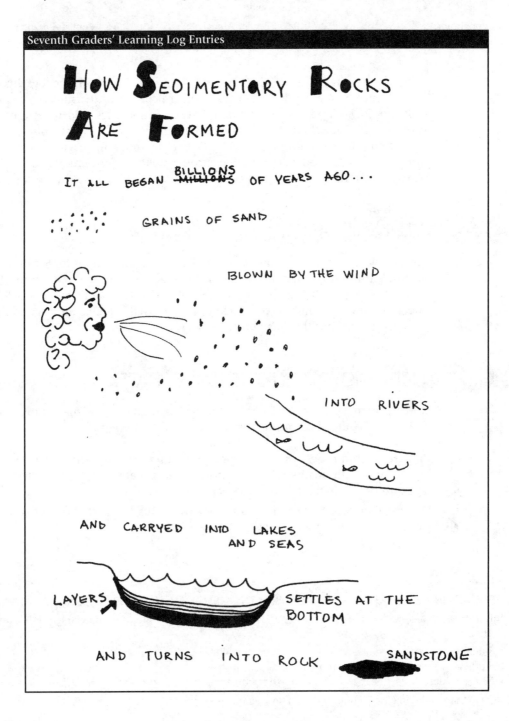

Seventh Graders' Learning Log Entries

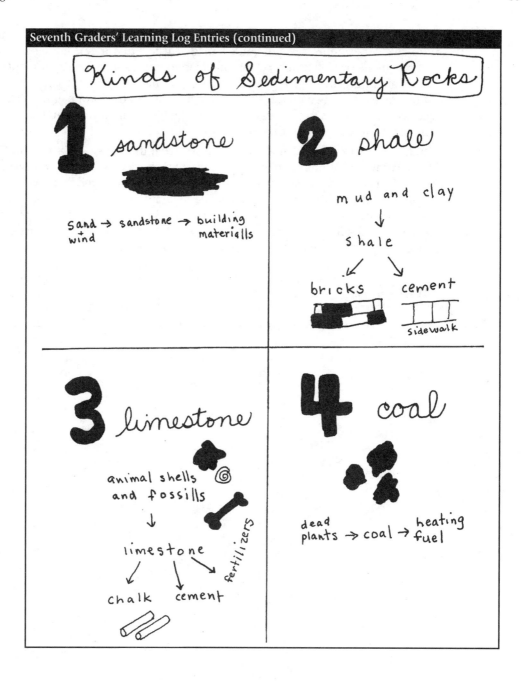

Seventh Graders' Learning Log Entries (continued)

Kinds of Sedimentary Rocks

1 sandstone

sand → sandstone → building
+   materialls
wind

2 shale

mud and clay
↓
shale
↙   ↘
bricks   cement

sidewalk

3 limestone

animal shells
and fossills
↓
limestone
↙   ↓   ↘
chalk   cement   fertilizers

4 coal

dead
plants → coal → heating
fuel

diagrams in learning logs. During a social studies unit on pioneers, for example, students do these activities in learning logs:

- Write questions to investigate during the unit
- Draw pictures of covered wagons
- List items the pioneers carried west
- Mark the Oregon Trail on a map of the United States
- Make clusters of information read in books
- Write responses to videos about pioneers
- Write a rough draft of a poem about life on the Oregon Trail
- Write a letter to the teacher at the end of the unit listing the five most important things they learned

Learning logs are used for similar purposes in science units. During a unit on rocks and minerals, for example, seventh graders made clusters that they completed as they read a chapter in the science textbook, compiled lab reports as they did experiments, did quick-writes after watching videos, and drew diagrams and charts about scientific information. Students made the two entries shown on pages 68 and 69. In one entry, a student used a series of illustrations to explain how sedimentary rocks are formed; in the other, a student charted the four types of sedimentary rocks.

Students also use learning logs to write about what they're learning in math: They record explanations and examples of concepts presented in class, write story problems, and react to mathematical concepts they're learning and to any problems they may be having. For example, during a unit on fractions, students draw diagrams of various fractions, write story problems using fractions, and quickwrite to explore the big ideas they're learning. Some upper grade teachers allow students the last 5 minutes of math class to summarize the day's lesson and to react to it in their learning logs.

REFERENCE

Strong, W. (2006). *Write for insight: Empowering content area learning, grades 6–12*. Boston: Allyn & Bacon/Pearson.

24 Making Words

Instructional Focus		Grade Levels
☐ Oral Language	☐ Comprehension	☑ PreK–Grade 2
☑ Phonemic Awareness/Phonics	☐ Writing	☑ Grades 3–5
☐ Fluency	☑ Spelling	☐ Grades 6–8
☐ Vocabulary	☐ Content Areas	☑ English Learners

Making words is an activity in which students arrange letter cards to spell words. Teachers choose words from books students are reading that exemplify particular phonics concepts or spelling patterns for students to practice. Then they prepare a set of letter cards that small groups or individual students can use to spell words. The teacher leads students as they create words using the letters. For example, after reading *Diary of a Spider* (Cronin, 2005), a group of first graders built these short-*i* and long-*i* words using the letters in the word *spider: is, sip, rip, dip, drip, side, ride,* and *ripe.* After spelling these words, children used all of the letters to spell the chosen word—*spider.*

WHY USE THIS INSTRUCTIONAL STRATEGY

Making words is an excellent teacher-directed spelling activity (Cunningham & Cunningham, 1992; Gunning, 1995). As students make words, they practice what they're learning about sound–symbol correspondences and spelling patterns. Teachers get feedback on what students understand; correct confusions; and review phonics concepts, spelling patterns, and affixes, when necessary.

Scaffolding English Learners

Teachers often use this instructional strategy with small groups of English learners to practice spelling patterns and rules. It's effective because students collaborate with classmates, and the activity is both nonthreatening and hands-on. Sometimes teachers bring together a group of English learners to do a word-making activity as a preview before doing it with the whole class (or afterward as a review), and sometimes they choose a different word to use that reinforces a spelling pattern these students are learning.

COMMON CORE STATE STANDARDS FOR ENGLISH LANGUAGE ARTS: *MAKING WORDS*

This instructional strategy supports these Common Core State Standards for Reading: Foundational Skills and Language:

• Students apply grade-level phonics and word-analysis skills.
• Students spell grade-appropriate words correctly.

Students apply phonics knowledge and word-analysis skills to spelling when they participate in making words activities.

HOW TO USE THIS INSTRUCTIONAL STRATEGY

Teachers usually work with the whole class for a making words activity; sometimes students work individually to arrange the letter cards to spell words, and at other times, they work with partners or in a small group. Here are the steps in this procedure:

1 **Make letter cards.** Teachers prepare a set of small letter cards with multiple copies of each letter; they make more copies of common letters, such as *a, e, i, r, s,* and *t.* They print the lowercase letterform on one side and the uppercase form on the reverse and package the cards letter by letter in small plastic bags or partitioned plastic boxes.

2 **Choose a word.** Teachers choose a word to use in the word-making activity and without disclosing the chosen word, have a student distribute the needed letter cards to classmates.

3 **Name the letter cards.** Teachers ask students to name the letter cards and arrange them on their desks with consonants in one group and vowels in another.

4 **Make words.** Students use the letter cards to spell words containing two, three, four, five, six, or more letters and list the words they can spell on a chart. Teachers monitor students' work and encourage them to fix misspelled words.

5 **Share words.** Teachers have students identify two-letter words they made and continue to report longer and longer words until they identify the chosen word made using every letter card. After students share all of the words, teachers suggest any words they missed and point out recently taught spelling patterns.

WHEN TO USE THIS INSTRUCTIONAL STRATEGY

Teachers choose words for word-making lessons from books they're reading with students. For example, after the class reads Eric Carle's *A House for Hermit Crab* (2005), *hermit crabs* offers many word-making possibilities; and for Laura Numeroff's *Chimps Don't Wear Glasses* (2006), *chimpanzee* works well. Upper grade teachers also choose words and phrases from chapter books they're reading for word-making activities; for *Number the Stars* (Lowry, 2011), *resistance fighters* can be used, and for *Tuck Everlasting* (Babbitt, 2007) or *Bridge to Terabithia* (Paterson, 2006), the title works well. Teachers can also identify other suitable words for word-making activities using two books that Patricia Cunningham and Dorothy Hall have compiled (1994a, 1994b).

A third grade teacher passed out the letters cards to spell *feather* after reading *Don't Fidget a Feather!* (Silverman, 1994). First, she asked students to make all of the two-letter words that they could; they spelled *he* and *at,* and she wrote the words on a chart. Then she asked them to make three-letter words, and they spelled *are, eat, art, fat, rat, hat, the, ate,* and *her;* she added these words to the chart. Then she asked students to spell *ear* and to substitute beginning sounds to spell *hear, fear,* and *tear.* Next, she asked them for another way to spell *hear,* and they spelled *here.* Then she asked students to add a letter to spell *heart.* They noticed that *heart* is made of two small words, *he* and *art.* The teacher also added all of these words to the chart, as shown on the next page. Finally, students spelled *father,* using all of the letters except one of the *e*'s, and then the teacher asked them to find a way to add the remaining *e*; they spelled *feather* and commented that the *ea* spelling represents a short-*e* sound. After the whole-class activity, the teacher placed a set of letter cards in a literacy center so that students could practice making words with the letters in *feather,* referring to the chart she made whenever necessary.

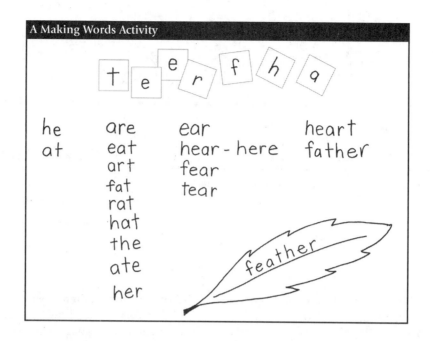

A Making Words Activity

t e e r f h a

he	are	ear	heart
at	eat	hear - here	father
	art	fear	
	fat	tear	
	rat		
	hat		
	the		
	ate		
	her		

feather

Differentiating Instruction

Making words is a hands-on activity that teachers use to provide guided practice on phonics, spelling, and morphemic analysis concepts that students are learning. They individualize instruction and meet students' needs in these ways:

- Students repeat a making words activity that they've already done with teacher guidance at a learning center, and they check their work using the chart the class compiled.

- Students arrange word cards to practice spelling high-frequency words they're learning, homophones, and words on weekly spelling lists.

- Students examine rhyming words and spelling patterns by using letter cards to spell words, for example: *bring, ding, spring, thing,* and *wing.*

- Students arrange prefix, suffix, and root word cards to make words, such as *dis + appear, hemi + sphere, journal + ist,* and *annoy + ance.*

Through these adaptations, students learn more about written language and gain confidence in themselves as writers.

REFERENCES

Babbitt, N. (2007). *Tuck everlasting.* New York: Square Fish Books.

Carle, E. (2005). *A house for hermit crab.* New York: Aladdin Books.

Cronin, D. (2005). *Diary of a spider.* New York: HarperCollins.

Cunningham, P. M., & Cunningham, J. W. (1992). Making words: Enhancing the invented spelling-decoding connection. *The Reading Teacher, 46,* 106–115.

Cunningham, P. M., & Hall, D. P. (1994a). *Making big words.* Parsippany, NJ: Good Apple.

Cunningham, P. M., & Hall, D. P. (1994b). *Making words.* Parsippany, NJ: Good Apple.

Gunning, T. G. (1995). Word building: A strategic approach to the teaching of phonics. *The Reading Teacher, 48,* 484–488.

Lowry, L. (2011). *Number the stars.* New York: Sandpiper.

Numeroff, L. (2006). *Chimps don't wear glasses.* New York: Aladdin Books.

Paterson, K. (2006). *Bridge to Terabithia.* New York: HarperCollins.

Silverman, E. (1994). *Don't fidget a feather!* New York: Simon & Schuster.

25 Minilessons

Instructional Focus		Grade Levels
☐ Oral Language	☑ Comprehension	☑ PreK–Grade 2
☑ Phonemic Awareness/Phonics	☑ Writing	☑ Grades 3–5
☑ Fluency	☑ Spelling	☑ Grades 6–8
☑ Vocabulary	☐ Content Areas	☑ English Learners

Teachers teach short, focused lessons called *minilessons* on literacy strategies and skills (Atwell, 1998; Hoyt, 2000). Topics for minilessons include how to write an entry in a reading log (see p. 113), find examples of figurative language in a text, use commas in a series, draw inferences, and combine sentences. In these lessons, teachers introduce a topic and connect it to the reading or writing students are doing, provide information, and supervise students as they practice. Minilessons usually last 15 to 30 minutes, but sometimes teachers extend the lesson over several days as students apply the topic in reading and writing activities. The best time to teach a minilesson is when students will have immediate opportunities to apply what they're learning.

Topics grow out of what students need to know to participate successfully in literacy activities as well as state-mandated grade-level standards or competencies. Mazzoni and Gambrell (2003) recommend that a whole-part-whole sequence be used to ensure that the instruction is meaningful and that students will be able to apply the topics they learn independently: The literacy activity is the first *whole*, the minilesson is the *part*, and having students apply what they're learning in other literacy activities is the second *whole*.

WHY USE THIS INSTRUCTIONAL STRATEGY

It's not enough to simply explain procedures, concepts, and strategies or remind students to use them; minilessons are an effective way to teach students how to actually use them. Teachers must actively engage students, encourage and scaffold them while they're learning, and then gradually withdraw their support (Dorn & Soffos, 2001).

COMMON CORE STATE STANDARDS FOR ENGLISH LANGUAGE ARTS: *MINILESSONS*

This instructional strategy supports all Common Core State Standards:
- Students apply knowledge about genres and structures.
- Students develop print concepts, phonological awareness, phonics, and word-identification skills.
- Students use Standard English conventions, grammar, and vocabulary.
- Students apply the writing process to produce effective compositions.

Students learn strategies, skills, and procedures through minilessons.

Scaffolding English Learners

Minilessons are especially important for English learners because they need a combination of direct instruction and supervised practice as they learn to speak, read, and write English at the same time. Teachers bring students together in small groups for minilessons so that they can clearly explain a topic, use pictures and objects, integrate hands-on activities, and provide opportunities for English learners to examine familiar texts and practice what they're learning together with classmates.

HOW TO USE THIS INSTRUCTIONAL STRATEGY

Teachers present minilessons to small groups of students and to the whole class on a wide variety of literacy topics using this procedure:

1. **Introduce the topic.** Teachers introduce the strategy or skill by naming it and making a connection between the topic and ongoing activities in the classroom.

2. **Share examples.** Teachers show how to use the topic with examples from students' own writing or from books students are reading.

3. **Provide information.** Teachers provide information, explaining and demonstrating the strategy or skill.

Steps in Teaching Three Minilessons

Step	*-ing* Inflectional Ending	Open-Mind Portraits	Homophones
1. Introduce the Topic	Explain that *-ing* is an inflectional ending, like *-ed* and *-s*.	Explain that open-mind portraits help students think more deeply about a character.	Remind students that homophones are words that sound alike but are spelled differently.
2. Share Examples	Have students "read the classroom" to locate examples of words with *-ing* endings and create a chart listing these words.	Show a sample open-mind portrait of a character from a book that students have already read.	Have students make a list of homophones. Have them share mnemonic devices for remembering when to use each word.
3. Provide Information	Reread the chart and have students circle each root word. Explain that the final consonant in short-vowel words is doubled before adding the ending.	Demonstrate how to make an open-mind portrait. List the steps on a chart that students can refer to as they make these portraits.	Have students create personal lists of the homophones they often confuse that they can refer to as they edit their writing.
4. Supervise Practice	Have students create booklets of *-ing* words and draw circles around the root words.	Have students work in small groups to make an open-mind portrait about a main character in a book they're reading.	Have students review their rough drafts to locate and correct any homophone errors they've made.
5. Assess Learning	Have students locate other words with the *-ing* ending in the books they're reading or writing.	Have students share their portraits and talk about how this activity helped them delve into the character's thoughts and actions.	Check students' next composition for homophone errors; if any are found, have students think of ways to remember which word to use.

4 **Supervise practice.** Students practice using the strategy or skill with teacher supervision.

5 **Assess learning.** Teachers monitor students' progress and evaluate their use of the newly learned strategy or skill.

WHEN TO USE THIS INSTRUCTIONAL STRATEGY

Teachers teach minilessons on a variety of literacy strategies and skills as a part of literature focus units, reading and writing workshop, and other instructional approaches. The box on page 75 shows how teachers follow the procedure to teach three minilessons. The first example is a minilesson to teach second graders about the *-ing* inflectional ending; the second teaches fourth graders how to make open-mind portraits (see p. 77) of characters; and the third minilesson reviews homophones for sixth graders.

REFERENCES

Atwell, N. (1998). *In the middle: New understandings about writing, reading, and learning.* Portsmouth, NH: Heinemann/Boynton/Cook.

Dorn, L. J., & Soffos, C. (2001). *Shaping literate minds: Developing self-regulated learners.* York, ME: Stenhouse.

Hoyt, L. (2000). *Snapshots.* Portsmouth, NH: Heinemann.

Mazzoni, S. A., & Gambrell, L. B. (2003). Principles of best practice: Finding common ground. In L. M. Morrow, L. B. Gambrell, & M. Pressley (Eds.), *Best practices in literacy instruction* (pp. 9–21). New York: Guilford Press.

26 Open-Mind Portraits

Instructional Focus

☐ Oral Language		☑ Comprehension		
☐ Phonemic Awareness/Phonics		☐ Writing		
☐ Fluency		☐ Spelling		
☐ Vocabulary		☐ Content Areas		

Grade Levels

☐ PreK–Grade 2
☑ Grades 3–5
☑ Grades 6–8
☐ English Learners

To think more deeply about a character and reflect on story events from the character's viewpoint, students draw open-mind portraits of the character (McLaughlin & Allen, 2001). These portraits have two parts: the character's face on the top, "portrait" page, and several "thinking" pages showing the character's mind at pivotal points in the story. As students draw open-mind portraits, they are visually representing characters and their thoughts. The two pages of a fourth grader's open-mind portrait on Sarah, the mail-order bride in *Sarah, Plain and Tall* (MacLachlan, 2005), are shown on page 78. The words and pictures on the "thinking" page represent her thoughts at the end of the story.

WHY USE THIS INSTRUCTIONAL STRATEGY

Students make open-mind portraits to focus on the main character in stories they're reading (Tompkins, 2010). It's a powerful way to examine character because as students draw portraits, they recall the appearance details the author included in the story, and as they complete the "thinking" pages, they review story events and analyze the theme as they consider the character's activities and motivation.

HOW TO USE THIS INSTRUCTIONAL STRATEGY

Students make individual open-mind portraits while they're reading a story or immediately afterward and then share their portraits with classmates. Teachers follow this procedure:

1 **Make a portrait of a character.** Students draw and color a large portrait of the head and neck of a character in a story they're reading.

COMMON CORE STATE STANDARDS FOR ENGLISH LANGUAGE ARTS: *OPEN-MIND PORTRAITS*

This instructional strategy supports these Common Core State Standards for Reading: Literature:

• Students comprehend grade-appropriate literature.
• Students analyze a character, drawing on specific details in the text.
• Students explain how a series of chapters fit together to provide the overall structure of a story.

Students make open-mind portraits to understand literature they're reading.

A Fourth Grader's Open-Mind Portrait

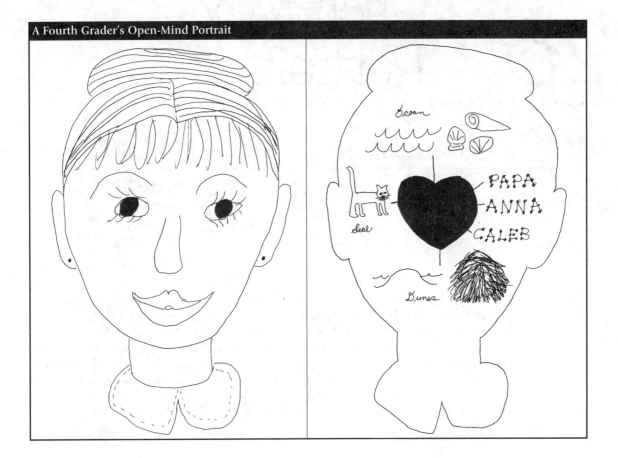

2 **Cut out the "portrait" and "thinking" pages.** Students cut out the portrait and attach it with a brad or staple on top of several more sheets of drawing paper. It's important that students place the fastener at the top of the portrait so that there's space available to draw and write on the "thinking" pages.

3 **Design the "thinking" pages.** Students lift the portrait and draw and write about the character's thoughts on the "thinking" pages. They show the character's thoughts at key points in the story.

4 **Share the completed open-mind portraits.** Students share their portraits with classmates and talk about the words and pictures they chose to include on the "thinking" pages.

WHEN TO USE THIS INSTRUCTIONAL STRATEGY

Students create open-mind portraits to think more deeply about a character in a story they're reading in literature focus units and literature circles. They often reread parts of the story to recall specific details about the character's appearance before they draw the portrait, and they may write several entries in a simulated journal to start thinking from that character's viewpoint before making the "thinking" pages of the open-mind portrait. In addition to making open-mind portraits of characters in stories they're reading, students can make open-mind portraits of historical figures as part of social studies units, and of well-known personalities after reading biographies (Paquette & Fello, 2010).

REFERENCES

MacLachlan, P. (2005). *Sarah, plain and tall.* New York: Scholastic.

McLaughlin, M., & Allen, M.B. (2001). *Guided comprehension: A teaching model for grades 3–8.* Newark, DE: International Reading Association.

Paquette, K. R., & Fello, S. E. (2010). Using open-mind portraits as a springboard to expository writing. *Childhood Education, 86,* 234–240.

Tompkins, G. E. (2010). *Literacy for the 21st century* (5th ed.). Boston: Allyn & Bacon/Pearson.

27　Plot Profiles

Instructional Focus		Grade Levels
☐ Oral Language	☑ Comprehension	☐ PreK–Grade 2
☐ Phonemic Awareness/Phonics	☐ Writing	☑ Grades 3–5
☐ Fluency	☐ Spelling	☑ Grades 6–8
☐ Vocabulary	☐ Content Areas	☐ English Learners

Students make plot profiles to examine the plot of a novel or chapter-book story. After reading each chapter, they mark a graph to track the tension or excitement of the story (Johnson & Louis, 1987). The box on the next page presents a plot profile for *Stone Fox* (Gardiner, 2003), a story about a boy who wins a dogsled race to save his grandfather's farm. Fourth graders met in small groups to talk about each chapter, and after these discussions, the whole class came together to decide how to mark the graph. At the end of the story, students analyzed the chart and rationalized that the tension dips in Chapters 3 and 7 because the story would be too stressful without these dips.

Teachers introduce plot profiles as they teach students about the plot development of a story. Students learn that *plot* is the sequence of events involving characters in conflict situations, and that a story's plot is based on the goals of one or more characters and how they go about attaining them. Chapter by chapter, as they read and mark a plot profile, students talk about plot development and the conflict situations characters are involved in. They also learn that *conflict* is the tension between the forces in the plot and that it's what interests readers enough to continue reading the story. They find examples of the different types of conflict—conflict between a character and nature, between a character and society, between characters, or within a character—in the stories they read (Lukens, 2007).

WHY USE THIS INSTRUCTIONAL STRATEGY

Plot profiles help students comprehend complex stories. By asking students to think about the conflict and tension in the story, teachers draw their attention back to this basic structure. Students read each chapter with a purpose in mind—understanding the conflict or tension. Then, as they talk about the story, students ask questions and offer comments, their classmates clarify misconceptions and offer comments, and all students' understanding of the story grows. At the end of the book, the plot profile provides a visual representation for students to use in appreciating their understanding of the plot.

COMMON CORE STATE STANDARDS FOR ENGLISH LANGUAGE ARTS: *PLOT PROFILES*

This instructional strategy supports these Common Core State Standards for Reading: Literature:

- Students comprehend grade-appropriate literature.
- Students compare and contrast events in a novel, citing details from the text.
- Students explain how chapters fit together to provide the overall structure of a story.

Students draw plot profiles to learn how authors organize novels.

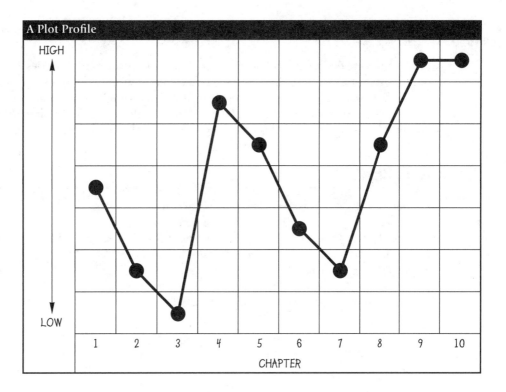

A Plot Profile

HIGH

LOW

1 2 3 4 5 6 7 8 9 10

CHAPTER

HOW TO USE THIS INSTRUCTIONAL STRATEGY

Students usually work together as a class to create a plot profile as they read and discuss a novel. Teachers follow this procedure as they guide students to think about the conflict in a story:

1 **Prepare the plot profile chart.** Teachers draw a large plot profile chart on chart paper to display in the classroom, with a column for each chapter and five to seven rows for the tension range. They also make small, individual copies of the plot profile for each student.

2 **Introduce the chart.** Teachers and students read and discuss the first chapter of the book; the discussion should focus on the plot development of the story and the tension in the chapter. Teachers may want to have students begin by discussing the chapter in small groups and then come together as a class to finish the discussion. Then teachers introduce the plot profile chart and explain that they'll make a graph on the chart to examine how the author developed the plot. Together the class decides on the level of tension in the first chapter and how they will mark the chart. One student marks the class chart, and all students mark their individual charts.

3 **Continue graphing the plot.** Students continue to read, discuss, and mark the tension of each chapter on the plot profile chart.

4 **Reflect on the chart.** After students finish reading the story and graphing the tension on the chart, they have a grand conversation (see p. 45) to discuss how the author developed the plot of the story. Teachers encourage students to think about the impact of the character's motivations on the conflict and story events. Students write a reflection about the story's plot development in their reading logs (see p. 113), or they write an essay to accompany their completed plot profiles.

WHEN TO USE THIS INSTRUCTIONAL STRATEGY

Plot profiles are designed for chapter-book stories, not picture-book stories, because picture books are shorter and usually aren't separated into sections as chapter books are. Chapter books in which main characters struggle to overcome great odds, or books in which there is a great deal of conflict, such as *Hatchet* (Paulsen, 2007), *Holes* (Sachar, 2008), *Princess Academy* (Hale, 2007), and *Shiloh* (Naylor, 2000), work well for plot profiles.

REFERENCES

Gardiner, J. R. (2003). *Stone Fox.* New York: Harper Trophy.

Hale, S. (2007). *Princess Academy.* New York: Bloomsbury.

Johnson, T. D., & Louis, D. R. (1987). *Literacy through literature.* Portsmouth, NH: Heinemann.

Lukens, R. J. (2007). *A critical handbook of children's literature* (8th ed.). Boston: Allyn & Bacon.

Naylor, P. R. (2000). *Shiloh.* New York: Aladdin Books.

Paulsen, G. (2007). *Hatchet.* New York: Simon & Schuster.

Sachar, L. (2008). *Holes.* New York: Farrar, Straus & Giroux.

28 Possible Sentences

Instructional Focus		Grade Levels
☐ Oral Language	☑ Comprehension	☐ PreK–Grade 2
☐ Phonemic Awareness/Phonics	☐ Writing	☑ Grades 3–5
☐ Fluency	☐ Spelling	☑ Grades 6–8
☑ Vocabulary	☑ Content Areas	☐ English Learners

Possible sentences is a prereading activity that activates students' background knowledge about content-area topics and related academic vocabulary (Blachowicz & Fisher, 2010; Lenski, Wham, & Johns, 1999). Students use what they know about a topic and their familiarity with English sentence structure to make predictions about word meanings and craft possible sentences; then after learning more, they review their sentences and make changes if they aren't accurate. This instructional procedure is typically used before reading nonfiction texts, especially content-area textbook chapters, but teachers also use it before giving oral presentations on social studies and science topics or viewing DVDs.

During a unit on the U.S. Constitution, an eighth grade teacher introduced this list of words:

amendment	legislative
branches of government	preamble
executive	ratify
federal	rights
judicial	suffrage

The students talked about the Constitution and these words briefly, but they needed more information so the teacher divided the class into small groups and gave each group one of these picture books to examine:

A More Perfect Union: The Story of Our Constitution (Maestro, 1990)

The United States Constitution and You (Sobel, 2001)

We the Kids: The Preamble to the Constitution of the United States (Catrow, 2005)

We the People: The Story of Our Constitution (Cheney, 2012)

After a few minutes, the class came back together to continue their discussion and define the words. One student recognized that *judicial* was related to judges; she could tell because

---

COMMON CORE STATE STANDARDS FOR ENGLISH LANGUAGE ARTS: *POSSIBLE SENTENCES*

This instructional strategy supports these Common Core State Standards for Language:

- Students use context as a clue to meaning.
- Students use Greek and Latin affixes and roots as clues to meaning.
- Students consult print and digital reference materials.

Students learn to determine the meaning of academic vocabulary through possible sentences activities.

she recognized the root word. Another joked that *ratify* is what happens to a rodent after it dies, but the majority of the class took their task seriously.

Next, they created these possible sentences:

⊙
The Constitution explains the 3 branches of government.

Amendments are new laws.

The branches of government are the executive, federal, judicial, and legislative.

The preamble of the Constitution begins "We the people of the United States."

The Constitution gives us rights to own guns and speak freely.

Massachusetts has a state legislative.

Government is like a tree with branches.

The judicial branch has judges.

We have rights to free speech, religion, and trials.

We have the right to suffrage.

GO DIGITAL

Word Cloud Generators
Word clouds are computer-generated dynamic arrangements of words. The words appearing most often in the text sample provided to the word cloud generator appear larger and are given more prominence than less frequently appearing words. Wordle (http://www.wordle.net) is the best known word cloud generator. It's quick and easy to use, and students can tweak clouds with varied fonts, layouts, and color schemes.

Some of the sentences are accurate, but others will be revised after students learn more. The sentences also demonstrate students' knowledge about parts of speech and sentence structure. The student who wrote about the branches of government explained that he had included *federal* as one branch because it was an adjective like *judicial*.

After learning more about the U.S. Constitution, the eighth graders created clusters (see p. 21) with information they'd found about each word. The cluster for *amendment*, for instance, included these words and numbers: *changes, ratified, unratified, abolish slavery #13, women's suffrage #19, Bill of Rights 1–10, Miranda Warning,* and *27.* Students also created a word cloud for the U.S. Constitution vocabulary using Wordle (http://www.wordle.net), an online word cloud generator.

WHY USE THIS INSTRUCTIONAL STRATEGY

Possible sentences is an effective vocabulary activity. Students activate their knowledge about content-area topics (Stahl & Kapinus, 1991). This instructional strategy teaches students to predict meanings of words, using their background knowledge, what they've learned about root words and affixes, and their knowledge about parts of speech and sentence structure. Students become more engaged and eager to learn because they want to determine whether their predictions are accurate.

HOW TO USE THIS INSTRUCTIONAL STRATEGY

Possible sentences is a whole-class activity that teachers use before giving an oral presentation or assigning a chapter in a content-area textbook. Teachers guide the class through the instructional strategy, but students work individually, with partners, or in small groups to compose and revise their possible sentences. This is the procedure:

1 **Choose words.** Teachers choose 8–10 key words related to a content-area topic. Students will probably be somewhat familiar with some words, but others are likely to be unfamiliar or used in a new way.

2 **Introduce the topic.** Teachers introduce the topic, making connections to topics previously studied, and asking students to share their ideas. If students have limited knowledge

about the topic and the vocabulary, teachers often read aloud a picture book on the topic or share photos or artifacts.

3 **Define the words.** Teachers have students define or explain the words. Upper grade students often group the words into related pairs.

4 **Write sentences.** Students compose sentences using each word or each related pair of words. Even though they're not sure about the meaning or how to use the words in sentences, they give it a try, they make a prediction, understanding that this possible sentence is like a rough draft; it can be revised later.

5 **Share the sentences.** Students share their possible sentences and talk about the plausibility of each one.

6 **Teach the lesson.** Students read the selection or listen to the presentation to test the accuracy of their predictions. They check their predictions by carefully reading the text selection.

7 **Evaluate the sentences.** Students evaluate the accuracy of their sentences and mark them as accurate (+), inaccurate (−), or don't know (?).

8 **Revise the inaccurate sentences.** Students revise the sentences that aren't accurate and share them with classmates.

WHEN TO USE THIS INSTRUCTIONAL STRATEGY

Teachers generally use the possible sentences activity during thematic units to introduce nonfiction topics and related vocabulary, but sometimes they use the activity before reading stories and novels. For example, when students are reading a book of historical fiction during a social studies unit, the possible sentences activity works especially well, linking stories and information. Students can also do a possible sentences activity as a project after reading a biography. For example, after reading a biography about Rosa Parks, a small group of sixth graders used these six words for a possible sentences activity with their classmates: *Civil Rights, equality, nonviolent, prejudice, refuse,* and *segregation.*

Differentiating Instruction

Possible sentences is a demanding activity because students must have a little background knowledge about the topic and be willing to make educated guesses about the meaning of academic vocabulary. Teachers can provide additional support for struggling students in these ways:

- Teachers give an oral presentation or share artifacts or photos before introducing the targeted words.
- Teachers have students talk about the topic with partners or in groups to share their knowledge.
- Teachers read aloud a picture book, have students view a DVD, or examine a website to introduce the concept before doing the possible sentences activity.
- Students examine picture books or photos related to the topic before beginning the possible sentences activity.
- Students take turns reading their sentences aloud and having classmates decide whether they're accurate.

Teachers also devise ways to extend the activity to challenge more advanced students, as the teacher did with the U.S. Constitution words.

REFERENCES

Blachowicz, C., & Fisher, P. J. (2010). *Teaching vocabulary in all classrooms* (4th ed.). Boston: Allyn & Bacon/Pearson.

Catrow, D. (2005). *We the kids: the Preamble to the Constitution of the United States.* New York: Puffin Books.

Cheney, L. (2012). *We the people: The story of our Constitution.* New York: Simon & Schuster.

Lenski, S. D., Wham, M. A., & Johns, J. L. (1999). *Reading and learning strategies for middle and high school students.* Dubuque, IA: Kendall/Hunt.

Maestro, B. (1990). *A more perfect union: The story of our Constitution.* New York: HarperCollins.

Sobel, S. (2001). *The United States Constitution and you.* New York: Barron's.

Stahl, S. A., & Kapinus, B. A. (1991). Possible sentences: Predicting word meanings to teach content area vocabulary. *The Reading Teacher, 45,* 36–45.

29 Prereading Plan

Instructional Focus		Grade Levels

Instructional Focus

- ☐ Oral Language
- ☐ Phonemic Awareness/Phonics
- ☐ Fluency
- ☑ Vocabulary

- ☑ Comprehension
- ☐ Writing
- ☐ Spelling
- ☑ Content Areas

Grade Levels

- ☐ PreK–Grade 2
- ☐ Grades 3–5
- ☑ Grades 6–8
- ☑ English Learners

Teachers use the prereading plan (PReP) to assess students' background knowledge in order to activate and (if necessary) build additional knowledge before students read nonfiction books and chapters in content-area textbooks (Langer, 1981; Vacca & Vacca, 2011). They introduce a key concept discussed in the reading assignment and ask students to brainstorm related words and ideas. Teachers and students talk about the concept, and afterward students quickwrite (see p. 99) to explore it. With this prereading preparation, students are better able to comprehend the reading assignment.

WHY USE THIS INSTRUCTIONAL STRATEGY

PReP is a prereading strategy that builds students' background knowledge and technical vocabulary and allows teachers to estimate students' knowledge about a topic. In addition, students' interest in the topic often increases as they participate in this activity.

Scaffolding English Learners

This activity is especially important for English learners who have limited background knowledge about a topic or technical vocabulary because it prepares them to read nonfiction books or content-area textbook chapters.

COMMON CORE STATE STANDARDS FOR ENGLISH LANGUAGE ARTS: *PREREADING PLAN*

This instructional strategy supports these Common Core State Standards for Reading: Informational Text and Language:

- Students identify the central idea and explain how details support it.
- Students integrate information presented visually with the print text.
- Students clarify the meaning of academic vocabulary.

Students use PReP to comprehend grade-appropriate nonfiction texts.

HOW TO USE THIS INSTRUCTIONAL STRATEGY

Teachers use this instructional strategy with the whole class or a small group of students who need additional support. Here is the procedure:

1 **Discuss a key concept.** Teachers introduce a key concept to students using a word, phrase, object, or picture to initiate a discussion.

2 **Brainstorm.** Teachers ask students to brainstorm words about the topic and record their ideas on a chart. They also help students make connections among the brainstormed ideas.

3 **Introduce vocabulary.** Teachers present additional vocabulary words that students need to read the assignment and clarify any misconceptions.

4 **Quickwrite about the topic.** Teachers have students draw pictures and/or quickwrite about the topic using words from the brainstormed list.

5 **Share the quickwrites.** Students share their quickwrites with the class, and teachers ask questions to help classmates clarify and elaborate their thinking.

6 **Read the assignment.** Students read the assignment and relate what they're reading to what they learned before reading.

WHEN TO USE THIS INSTRUCTIONAL STRATEGY

Teachers use this instructional strategy during thematic units. Before reading a social studies textbook chapter about the Bill of Rights, for example, an eighth grade teacher used PReP to introduce the concept that citizens have freedoms and responsibilities. Students brainstormed this list during a discussion of the Bill of Rights:

⊙ guaranteed in the Constitution
James Madison
1791
10 amendments
citizens
freedom of speech
freedom of religion
freedom to assemble
homes can't be searched without a search warrant
owning guns and pistols
limits on these freedoms for everyone's good
"life, liberty, and the pursuit of happiness"
act responsibly
vote intelligently
right to a jury trial
serve on juries
no cruel or unusual punishments
death penalty
power to the people
serve in public offices—city council, school board, legislature, president

Then students wrote quickwrites to make personal connections to the ideas they brainstormed before reading the chapter. Here is one student's quickwrite:

⦿ I always knew America was a free country but I thought it was because of the Declaration of Independence. Now I know that the Bill of Rights is a list of our freedoms. There are ten freedoms in the Bill of Rights. I have the freedom to go to any church I want, to own guns, to speak my mind, and to have newspapers. I never thought of serving on a jury as a freedom and my Mom didn't either. She was on a jury about a year ago and she didn't want to do it. It took a whole week and her boss didn't like her missing work. The trial was about someone who robbed a store and shot a man but he didn't die. I'm going to tell her that it is important to do jury duty. When I am an adult, I hope I get to be on a jury of a murder trial. I want to protect my freedoms and I know it is a citizen's responsibility, too.

When the teacher read this student's quickwrite, she identified several concepts that the class had discussed and noticed that the student confused the number of amendments with the number of freedoms listed in the amendments. She clarified some misunderstandings individually with students and mentioned others during class discussions.

REFERENCES

Langer, J. A. (1981). From theory to practice: A prereading plan. *Journal of Reading, 25,* 152–157.

Vacca, R. T., & Vacca, J. L. (2011). *Content area reading: Literacy and learning across the curriculum* (10th ed.). Boston: Allyn & Bacon/Pearson.

30 Process Drama

Instructional Focus		Grade Levels
☑ Oral Language	☑ Comprehension	☑ PreK–Grade 2
☐ Phonemic Awareness/Phonics	☐ Writing	☑ Grades 3–5
☐ Fluency	☐ Spelling	☑ Grades 6–8
☐ Vocabulary	☑ Content Areas	☑ English Learners

Process drama is an imaginative and spontaneous role-play activity in which students explore stories they're reading and social studies topics they're studying (O'Neill, 1995; Wagner, 1999). Teachers create an unscripted dramatic context about a story episode or a historical event, and the students assume roles to experience and reflect on the episode or event (Schneider & Jackson, 2000). Teachers have to think on their feet or reflect in action as the dramatization proceeds, dealing again and again with unique situations based on students' comments and reflections.

For example, while an eighth grade class was studying the Underground Railroad, the teacher created a dramatic context about the moment when a group of escaped slaves reach the Ohio River; they'll be safe once they cross the river, but they're not safe yet. It's important that the teacher focuses on a particularly critical moment—one that's tension filled or creates a dilemma. Most of the students play the role of escaped slaves, but others become conductors, guiding the slaves to safety, or Quakers who are risking their lives to hide the slaves. Several other students are bounty hunters or plantation owners, trying to capture the escaped slaves.

With everyone participating in a role, the teacher and students create an imaginary dramatic world, exploring the critical moment from their viewpoints. The teacher moves the action forward by framing the moment, recounting the event, and asking questions. After reliving the experience, students reflect on it by writing a simulated journal entry or letter from the viewpoint of the person they're portraying in the role-play activity; they share information about the experience and reflect on it. Afterward, students step out of their roles to discuss the experience and share what they've learned.

WHY USE THIS INSTRUCTIONAL STRATEGY

Process drama goes beyond improvisation; not only do the students reenact the episode or event, but they explore the topic from the viewpoint of a book character or a historical

---

COMMON CORE STATE STANDARDS FOR ENGLISH LANGUAGE ARTS: *PROCESS DRAMA*

This instructional strategy supports these Common Core State Standards for Reading: Literature, Reading: Informational Text, and Listening and Speaking:

- Students analyze the elements of story structure.
- Students integrate information presented in different formats.
- Students review ideas presented in discussions and draw conclusions.

Through process drama activities, students deepen their understanding of stories and nonfiction topics.

personality as they role-play, respond to the teacher's questions, and write journal entries or letters. The discussion that follows the reenactment also deepens students' understanding. This instructional strategy provides an opportunity for students to walk a mile in other people's shoes and see the world from their viewpoint (Schneider, Crumpler, & Rogers, 2006). Process drama is a valuable activity because it stimulates students' curiosity and makes them want to continue reading and learning more about historical events, and it encourages them to consider multiple perspectives (Wagner, 1999).

Scaffolding English Learners

Process drama is appropriate for English learners because this instructional strategy doesn't require English proficiency. The emphasis is on what students are doing and thinking during the role-play activity; it's the process, not the product, that counts. Process drama is based on dramatic play, and as students assume roles and participate in the activity, they become emotionally involved in the book they're reading or the social studies content they're learning. ELs can draw pictures or create other visual products to share their reflections, if they're not comfortable writing journal entries and participating in discussions.

HOW TO USE THIS INSTRUCTIONAL STRATEGY

Process drama is a whole-class activity, and teachers follow these steps to implement this procedure:

1 **Set the purpose.** Teachers identify the topic and set the purpose for the process drama activity.

2 **Establish the imaginary dramatic world.** Teachers explain the dramatic context for the activity, and everyone assumes a role. Sometimes teachers share artifacts they've collected that relate to the characters and the event.

3 **Dramatize the event.** Students participate in the dramatization, staying in the role of the character they've chosen and building on the experience. Teachers create layers of dramatic tension by presenting dilemmas and introducing multiple perspectives, and the students work through the problems as they role-play their characters.

4 **Ask questions.** Teachers ask questions or invite students to ask questions about the dramatic context, and then students respond to them, usually from the viewpoint of their characters.

5 **Prompt reflection.** Students write simulated journal entries or letters in the persona of their characters. They include details and insights they've gained through the dramatization.

6 **Discuss the activity.** Teachers and students talk about the dramatization, reflecting on the experience and sharing their writing to gain new insights.

WHEN TO USE THIS INSTRUCTIONAL STRATEGY

Teachers use process drama during literature focus units and thematic units to allow students to delve more deeply into a book they're reading or a social studies topic they're studying. For instance, to explore the themes and investigate the motivations of characters, fifth graders reading *Number the Stars* (Lowry, 2011), a World War II story about the evacuation of Jews from Nazi-occupied Denmark told from the viewpoint of a 10-year-old girl, take on the roles of Annemarie; her Jewish friend, Ellen; King Christian X; the Resistance fighters; the fishermen who transported the Jews to safety in Sweden; and Nazi soldiers. Teachers choose significant events for students to dramatize, such as when King Christian X wears a Jewish star on his uniform, when Ellen pretends to be Annemarie's sister, and when Annemarie delivers cocaine-soaked handkerchiefs to the fishermen who have hidden Jews on their ships.

REFERENCES

Lowry, L. (2011). *Number the stars*. New York: Sandpiper.

O'Neill, C. (1995). *Drama worlds: A framework for process drama*. Portsmouth, NH: Heinemann.

Schneider, J. J., Crumpler, T. P., & Rogers, T. (2006). *Process drama and multiple literacies*. Portsmouth, NH: Heinemann.

Schneider, J. J., & Jackson, S. A. W. (2000). Process drama: A special space and place for writing. *The Reading Teacher, 54*, 38–51.

Wagner, B. J. (1999). *Dorothy Heathcote: Drama as a learning medium* (Rev. ed.). Portsmouth, NH: Heinemann.

31 Question-Answer-Relationships

Instructional Focus		Grade Levels
☐ Oral Language	☑ Comprehension	☐ PreK–Grade 2
☐ Phonemic Awareness/Phonics	☐ Writing	☐ Grades 3–5
☐ Fluency	☐ Spelling	☑ Grades 6–8
☐ Vocabulary	☑ Content Areas	☑ English Learners

Taffy Raphael's Question-Answer-Relationships (QAR) procedure teaches students to be consciously aware of whether they're likely to find the answer to a comprehension question "right there" on the page, between the lines, or beyond the information provided in the text (Raphael, Highfield, & Au, 2006; Raphael & Wonnacott, 1985). By being aware of the requirements posed by a question, students are better able to answer it.

QAR differentiates among the types of questions and the kinds of thinking required to answer them: Some questions require only literal thinking, but others demand higher levels of thinking. Here are Raphael's four types of questions:

- **Right There Questions.** Readers find the answer "right there" in the text, usually in the same sentence as words from the question. These are literal-level questions.

- **Think and Search Questions.** The answer is in the text, but readers must search for it in different parts of the text and put the ideas together. These are inferential-level questions.

- **Author and Me Questions.** Readers use a combination of the author's ideas and their own ideas to answer the question. These questions combine inferential and application levels.

- **On My Own Questions.** Readers use their own ideas to answer the questions; sometimes it isn't even necessary to read the text to answer the question. These are application- and evaluation-level questions.

The first two types of questions are known as "in the book" questions because the answers can be found in the book, and the last two types are "in the head" (Raphael, 1986) questions because they require information and ideas not presented in the book. An eighth grader's chart describing these four types of questions is shown on page 94.

COMMON CORE STATE STANDARDS FOR ENGLISH LANGUAGE ARTS: *QUESTION-ANSWER-RELATIONSHIPS*

This instructional strategy supports these Common Core State Standards for Reading: Informational Text:

- Students answer questions to demonstrate their understanding of nonfiction texts.
- Students cite textual evidence to answer "right there," "think and search," and "author and me" questions.

Students use QAR to read and comprehend grade-appropriate informational texts.

An Eighth Grader's QAR Chart

ℚUESTIONS

RIGHT THERE — *The answer is easy to Find in the book. It is near the Question.*

THINK AND SEARCH — *The answer is in the book but it isn't all in one place. I have to search for it and put the parts together.*

AUTHOR AND ME — *The answer is a combination of Ideas in the book and my own Ideas.*

ON MY OWN — *The answer is NOT in the book. I have to do my own thinking.*

WHY USE THIS INSTRUCTIONAL STRATEGY

The goal of QAR is for students to become more aware of the strategic nature of comprehension. After practicing the strategy, students are encouraged to apply it when they're reading both narrative and expository texts and when answering comprehension questions independently. In addition, QAR prepares students to answer the comprehension questions on high-stakes achievement tests.

HOW TO USE THIS INSTRUCTIONAL STRATEGY

Students work together as a class, in small groups, or individually to identify the types of questions before reading and then usually read and answer the questions individually. Teachers follow these steps as they use the QAR strategy:

1. **Read the questions before reading the text.** Students read the questions before reading the text to get an idea of what to think about as they read.

2. **Predict how to answer the questions.** Students consider which of the four types of questions each question represents and the level of thinking required to answer each one.

3. **Read the text.** Students read the text while thinking about the questions they'll answer afterward.

4. **Answer the questions.** Students reread the questions, determine where to find the answers, locate the answers, and write them.

5. **Share answers.** Students share their answers and explain how they answered the questions. They should again refer to the type of question and whether the answer was "in the book" or "in the head."

WHEN TO USE THIS INSTRUCTIONAL STRATEGY

Students use the QAR strategy whenever they're expected to answer questions after reading a story, nonfiction book, or chapter in a content-area textbook. They can also write their own "in the book" and "in the head" questions. An eighth grade teacher, for instance, asked his students to write examples of the four levels of questions in their reading logs (see p. 113) as they read novels during literature circles and literature focus units. As students were reading *The Giver* (Lowry, 2006), they wrote these questions and asked them during a grand conversation (see p. 45):

Right There Questions
What was the first color Jonas could see?
What does a Receiver do?
Who was Rosemary?

Think and Search Questions
What does "release" mean?
How is Jonas different than the other people?
Why did Rosemary ask to be released?

Author and Me Questions
What was wrong with Jonas's Mom and Dad?
What happened to Jonas and Gabe at the end of the book?
Was the Giver an honorable person?

On My Own Questions
Would you like to live in this community?
What would you have done if you were Jonas?
Could this happen in the United States?

Taffy Raphael and Katherine Au (2011a, 2011b, 2011c) have compiled three books of lessons to teach students how to answer QAR questions; one book is for second and third graders, another is for fourth and fifth graders, and another is for sixth through eighth graders. Students can also write questions when reading nonfiction books and chapters in content-area textbooks.

REFERENCES

Lowry, L. (2006). *The giver.* New York: Delacorte.

Raphael, T. E. (1986). Teaching question-answer-relationships, revisited. *The Reading Teacher, 39,* 516–523.

Raphael, T. E., & Au, K. H. (2011a). *QAR comprehension lessons: Grades 4–5.* New York: Scholastic.

Raphael, T. E., & Au, K. H. (2011b). *QAR comprehension lessons: Grades 6–8.* New York: Scholastic.

Raphael, T. E., & Au, K. H. (2011c). *QAR comprehension lessons: Grades 2–3.* New York: Scholastic.

Raphael, T. E., Highfield, K., & Au, K. H. (2006). *QAR now: A powerful and practical framework that develops comprehension and higher-level thinking in all students.* New York: Scholastic.

Raphael, T. E., & Wonnacott, C. A. (1985). Heightening fourth grade students' sensitivity to sources of information for answering comprehension questions. *Reading Research Quarterly, 20,* 282–296.

32 Questioning the Author

Instructional Focus		Grade Levels
☑ Oral Language	☑ Comprehension	☐ PreK–Grade 2
☐ Phonemic Awareness/Phonics	☐ Writing	☑ Grades 3–5
☐ Fluency	☐ Spelling	☑ Grades 6–8
☐ Vocabulary	☑ Content Areas	☐ English Learners

Isabel Beck and Margaret McKeown (2006) developed Questioning the Author (QtA) to teach students to ask questions and talk with classmates as they grapple with the complex ideas in texts they're reading. Students become actively involved in creating meaning as they break the text into smaller chunks and examine the ideas that the author presents. Students learn to view texts as fallible products written by authors who make errors and who sometimes don't write as clearly as they should. Once students understand this tenet of fallibility, they read texts differently. Too often, students assume that if they don't understand something they're reading, it's because they're not smart or don't read well enough: Unfortunately, they assume it's their fault.

Teachers teach students to ask questions that Beck and McKeown call "queries" and to discuss the text with classmates while they're reading to make sense of it. Queries are used to support students as they develop comprehension; conversely, traditional questions monitor students' recall of facts. Sometimes the focus in these whole-class discussions is on a single sentence, and at other times, it's on a paragraph or longer chunk of text. Teachers and students ask queries such as the following:

- What's the author trying to tell us here?
- What's the author talking about here?
- How does this fit with what the author told us before?
- Why is the author telling us this?

As students respond to open-ended queries like these, they share ideas and work with the teacher and classmates to construct meaning.

Teachers use six discussion moves as they orchestrate the discussion:

Marking. Teachers draw attention to particular ideas students have expressed.

Turning-back. Teachers return responsibility for exploring the text to students and students' attention back to the text.

COMMON CORE STATE STANDARDS FOR ENGLISH LANGUAGE ARTS: *QUESTIONING THE AUTHOR*

This instructional strategy supports these Common Core State Standards for Reading: Literature and Reading: Informational Text:

- Students read grade-appropriate stories and nonfiction texts.
- Students explain what a text says explicitly and draw inferences.
- Students examine how authors support their viewpoints.

Students use Questioning the Author as a comprehension tool.

Revoicing. Teachers interpret and rephrase students' ideas that they're struggling to express.

Recapping. Teachers summarize the big ideas in order to move ahead in the text.

Modeling. Teachers share their thinking as they talk about a point students may have missed.

Annotating. Teachers provide information during a discussion. (Beck & McKeown, 2006)

In these discussions, teachers and students work together to build meaning. Teachers prompt students to think more deeply, and they manage the discussion, but they should do less talking than the students do.

WHY USE THIS INSTRUCTIONAL STRATEGY

Teachers use QtA to expand students' thinking about a text; it's useful for developing higher level thinking (Beck, McKeown, Hamilton, & Kucan, 1997; Liang & Dole, 2006). The goal is for students to internalize this strategy and to use it whenever they're reading. In addition, the discussions are motivational because they get students engaged with the text.

HOW TO USE THIS INSTRUCTIONAL STRATEGY

Teachers use QtA with the whole class, and they follow this procedure:

1 **Analyze the text.** Teachers identify the big ideas in the text that they want students to focus on and decide how to segment the text to facilitate students' comprehension.

2 **Develop queries.** Teachers brainstorm a list of queries to ask about the big ideas in each segment. For example: "What's the author trying to tell us?" and "Why did the author say _____?" These queries are used to encourage students to probe the ideas, facilitate their discussion, and extend their understanding. Teachers often jot queries on self-stick notes that they place in their copy of the book students are reading.

3 **Read the text.** Students read the first segment of text, stopping at a predetermined point to talk about what they've read.

4 **Ask queries.** Teachers present a query to begin the discussion. Students respond by sharing their interpretations, rereading excerpts from the text, questioning ideas, clarifying confusions, and talking together to deepen their understanding. Teachers orchestrate the discussion using marking, revoicing, modeling, and the other discussion moves, and they ask additional questions based on the students' comments, including "Do you agree with what _____ said?" and "How does this information connect with what you already know?"

5 **Continue reading and asking queries.** Teachers repeat steps 3 and 4 as students read and discuss each segment of text.

6 **Discuss the text.** Teachers lead a discussion based on students' responses to the queries to bring closure to the reading experience. They raise issues of accuracy and viewpoint; invite students to make personal, world, and textual connections; and compare this text to other books on the same topic or by the same author.

WHEN TO USE THIS INSTRUCTIONAL STRATEGY

Teachers explain the central tenet of QtA, that authors and their texts are fallible, at the beginning of the school year to give students more confidence in their ability to read and understand books. They also teach students how to ask queries and talk about a text so that they're ready to use QtA whenever they're reading difficult narrative and expository texts. Teachers use this strategy during literature focus units or literature circles whenever students have difficulty understanding a particular passage, and during thematic units when students are reading chapters in content-area textbooks and other nonfiction books.

REFERENCES

Beck, I. L., & McKeown, M. G. (2006). *Improving comprehension with questioning the author: A fresh and expanded view of a powerful approach.* New York: Scholastic.

Beck, I. L., McKeown, M. G., Hamilton, R., & Kucan, L. (1997). *Questioning the author: An approach for enhancing student engagement with text.* Newark, DE: International Reading Association.

Liang, L. A., & Dole, J. A. (2006). Help with teaching reading comprehension: Comprehension instructional frameworks. *The Reading Teacher, 59,* 742–753.

33 Quickwrites

....

Instructional Focus		Grade Levels
☐ Oral Language	☑ Comprehension	☐ PreK–Grade 2
☐ Phonemic Awareness/Phonics	☑ Writing	☑ Grades 3–5
☐ Fluency	☐ Spelling	☑ Grades 6–8
☐ Vocabulary	☑ Content Areas	☑ English Learners

Quickwrites are impromptu writings that students use to explore a topic or respond to a question (Brozo & Simpson, 2007; Readence, Bean, & Baldwin, 2005). They write for 5 to 10 minutes, letting their thoughts flow without stopping to make revisions or correct misspelled words. The focus is on generating ideas and developing writing fluency. Students think about ideas, reflect on what they know about a topic, ramble on paper, and make connections among ideas. Here's a series of quickwrites that a fifth grader wrote as she listened to her teacher read aloud *The Higher Power of Lucky* (Patron, 2006), an award-winning story of a plucky 10-year-old girl named Lucky who tries to surmount her problems and bring stability to her life:

Prompt: Why do you think the main character is named Lucky?

◉ I don't know. At this point I don't think Lucky is lucky at all. Her mom died and her dad doesn't want her. She seems pretty unlucky. All that I can think is that Lucky is going to get more lucky at the end of the book. I hope something really good happens to her because she deserves it.

Prompt: Do you think Brigitte will abandon Lucky?

◉ Lucky is really afraid that Brigitte will go back home to Paris. I don't think Brigitte is going to leave. It would be a really mean thing to do and Brigitte is sort of a mom and moms don't do that. I also think it's bad for a girl to have to worry about being abandoned. That's really sad. I predict that Lucky will have a real family at the end of the book.

Prompt: What happened when Lucky hit bottom?

◉ It happened when she ran away from home. There was a bad dust storm and Miles was lost and it was her fault Miles got lost. She was wearing Brigitte's beautiful red dress and she ruined it. I thought she'd get in big trouble and maybe she'd even die and so would Miles and her dog but it didn't happen that way. Everybody in town drove their cars out to the caves to find her and they were so happy to see her and Miles that they didn't even get mad. Lots of good things happened. Best of all, she found out that Brigitte was going to adopt her and would always be her mom. I love this book.

....

COMMON CORE STATE STANDARDS FOR ENGLISH LANGUAGE ARTS: *QUICKWRITES*

This instructional strategy supports these Common Core State Standards for Reading: Informational Text, Writing, and Language:

- Students integrate information presented in different media and formats to understand a topic.
- Students summarize relevant information.
- Students apply grade-appropriate academic vocabulary.

Students do quickwrites to integrate ideas and vocabulary they're learning.

The students in this class wrote their quickwrites after their teacher finished reading each chapter or two and before they began to talk about the story in grand conversations (see p. 45). The quickwrites helped them reflect on the story and prepare for the discussions.

WHY USE THIS INSTRUCTIONAL STRATEGY

Quickwriting is similar to freewriting, a writing strategy popularized by Peter Elbow (1998) as a way to help students explore and develop ideas. Elbow's emphasis was on content rather than mechanics. Even by third grade, students have learned that many teachers emphasize correct spelling and careful handwriting more than the content of a composition. Elbow explains that focusing on mechanics makes writing "dead" because it doesn't allow students' natural voices to come through.

Scaffolding English Learners

Quickwriting is an effective instructional strategy for English learners because the writing is personal and the emphasis is on exploring ideas rather than on mechanical correctness. Sometimes English learners who have difficulty writing in English do "quickdraws" and use illustrations or a combination of illustrations and words to explore ideas.

HOW TO USE THIS INSTRUCTIONAL STRATEGY

Teacher-directed quickwrites are a whole-class activity. Students each do their own quickwrite and then share in small groups and later with the class. Here is the procedure:

1 **Choose a topic.** Students choose a topic or question (or the teacher assigns one) for the quickwrite, and they write it at the top of their papers.

2 **Write about the topic.** Students write sentences and paragraphs to brainstorm ideas and explore the topic for 5 to 10 minutes. They focus on interesting ideas, make connections between the topic and their own lives and the world around them, and reflect on their reading or learning. They rarely, if ever, stop writing to reread or correct errors in what they've written.

3 **Read quickwrites.** Students meet in small groups to read their quickwrites, and then one student in each group is chosen to share with the class. That student rereads his or her quickwrite in preparation for sharing with the class and adds any missing words and completes any unfinished thoughts.

4 **Share chosen quickwrites.** Students in each group who have been chosen to share their quickwrites take turns reading them aloud.

5 **Write a second time.** Sometimes students write a second time, either on the same topic or on a new topic that emerged through writing and sharing; this second quickwrite is usually more focused than the first one. Or students can expand their first quickwrite after listening to classmates share their quickwrites or after learning more about the topic.

WHEN TO USE THIS INSTRUCTIONAL STRATEGY

Teachers use quickwriting to promote thinking during literature focus units and thematic units. It's used as a warm-up at the beginning of a lesson or to promote reflection at the end of a lesson, and sometimes students identify the topics or questions for the

A Sixth Grader's Quickwrite

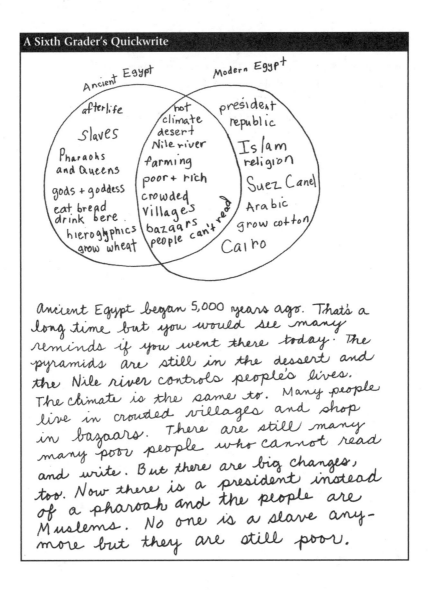

Ancient Egypt / Modern Egypt

afterlife
slaves
Pharaohs and Queens
gods + goddess
eat bread
drink bere
hieroglyphics
grow wheat

hot climate
desert
Nile river
farming
poor + rich
crowded villages
bazaars
people can't read

president republic
Islam religion
Suez Canel
Arabic
grow cotton
Cairo

Ancient Egypt began 5,000 years ago. That's a long time but you would see many reminds if you went there today. The pyramids are still in the dessert and the Nile river controls people's lives. The climate is the same to. Many people live in crouded villages and shop in bazaars. There are still many many poor people who cannot read and write. But there are big changes, too. Now there is a president instead of a pharoah and the people are Muslems. No one is a slave anymore but they are still poor.

quickwrite. The box above shows a sixth grader's quickwrite during a unit on ancient Egypt, which was written after a discussion comparing ancient and modern Egypt. As the class compared ancient and modern Egypt, the teacher made a Venn diagram (see p. 144) on chart paper; then students each made their own Venn diagram and referred to it as they wrote their quickwrites. In the quickwrite, the student began by writing about the "reminders" of ancient Egypt that can be seen today; after listing some of the ways that the two Egypts are alike, the student focused on a few of the differences. The purpose was to reinforce what students are learning, not to write a comparison-contrast essay.

Quickwrites are also an effective prewriting strategy (Routman, 2004). Before beginning to write, students often do several quickwrites to explore what they know about a topic. They brainstorm ideas and vocabulary, play with language, and identify ideas they need to learn more about before moving on to the drafting stage.

REFERENCES

Brozo, W. G., & Simpson, M. L. (2007). *Content literacy for today's adolescents: Honoring diversity and building competence* (5th ed.). Upper Saddle River, NJ: Merrill/Prentice Hall.

Elbow, P. (1998). *Writing without teachers* (25th anniversary ed.). New York: Oxford University Press.

Patron, S. (2006). *The higher power of Lucky*. New York: Atheneum.

Readence, J. E., Bean, T. W., & Baldwin, R. S. (2005). *Content area literacy: An integrated approach* (8th ed.). Dubuque, IA: Kendall/Hunt.

Routman, R. (2004). *Writing essentials: Raising expectations and results while simplifying teaching*. Portsmouth, NH: Heinemann.

34 Quilts

....

Instructional Focus		Grade Levels
☐ Oral Language	☑ Comprehension	☐ PreK–Grade 2
☐ Phonemic Awareness/Phonics	☐ Writing	☑ Grades 3–5
☐ Fluency	☐ Spelling	☑ Grades 6–8
☐ Vocabulary	☑ Content Areas	☑ English Learners

Students make quilt squares to extend their comprehension and to celebrate a story that they've read or a topic they've studied (Tompkins, 2013). They cut out construction paper squares, draw pictures in one section and add decorations in other sections, and arrange the squares to look like a quilt. Sometimes students copy a quote, record a fact, or write a poem or other piece of writing in a section or around the outside of the square. In this visual activity, students often choose designs and colors for their quilts that emphasize a theme or big idea. After reading *Princess Academy* (Hale, 2007), a Newbery Honor book about a poor mountain girl named Miri who learns to appreciate herself as she saves the girls at her school and in her village, a sixth grader made the quilt square that's presented on page 104. The triangle behind the circle represents Mt. Eskel, the mountain community where Miri lives; the circle represents Miri's journey to self-acceptance; the heart represents Miri's love for her village; and the flower in the middle of the heart is the Miri flower—her namesake. Notice that the flower has three blossoms, one for her father, her sister, and her boyfriend, Peder.

Quilts are a cultural phenomenon in America and around the world: Black slaves used them as maps to freedom in the early 1800s, pioneers carried memory quilts when they traveled west in covered wagons, and immigrants brought them to Ellis Island. More recently, the Hmong people from Southeast Asia used quiltlike story cloths to tell about their escape from their home countries. Latin American *arpilleras* are similar quiltlike wall hangings that use cloth pictures to tell a story. Others have created art quilts to share stories and information. Many picture books and novels tell stories about quilts and use quilts as illustrations; for example, Susan Kirby's series of American Quilts stories, including *Ellen's Story* (2000) and *Daniel's Story* (2001), prove that families, like quilts, can be pieced together in different ways. The Booklist feature on page 104 shows the range of quilt books that are available to share with students today. Students get ideas for the quilts they want to make from these stories, and they learn more about quilt patterns from nonfiction books, such as Mary Cobb's *The Quilt-Block History of Pioneer Days: With Projects Kids Can Make* (1995), that are also available.

....

COMMON CORE STATE STANDARDS FOR ENGLISH LANGUAGE ARTS: *QUILTS*

This instructional strategy supports these Common Core State Standards for Reading: Literature and Reading: Informational Text:

- Students integrate information presented in varied media and formats to understand a topic.
- Students determine the theme of a story.
- Students analyze how visual elements contribute to meaning.

Students make quilt squares to integrate their knowledge and celebrate their learning.

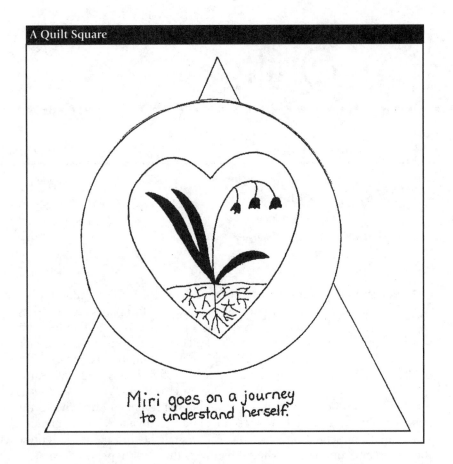

A Quilt Square

Miri goes on a journey to understand herself.

WHY USE THIS INSTRUCTIONAL STRATEGY

The language arts involve more than the four traditional modes of listening, speaking, reading, and writing; they also include two visual modes—viewing and visually representing. Students have the opportunity to use these visual modes as they create quilt squares

BOOKLIST
Quilt Books

Brumbeau, J. (2001). *The quiltmaker's gift.* New York: Scholastic. PM (fable)

Cha, K. (1998). *Dia's story cloth.* New York: Lee & Low. M (Hmong story cloth)

Coerr, E. (1989). *The Josefina story quilt.* New York: HarperCollins. P (pioneer)

Dorros, A. (1995). *Tonight is carnival.* New York: Puffin Books. P (Latin American *arpillera*)

Flournoy, J. (1996). *The patchwork quilt.* New York: Scholastic. PM (memory)

Gibbons, G. (2004). *The quilting bee.* New York: HarperCollins. PM (nonfiction)

Hopkinson, D. (2003). *Sweet Clara and the freedom quilt.* New York: Knopf. M (slavery-to-freedom)

Line, J. L. (2001). *Quilts from The Quiltmaker's Gift.* New York: Scholastic. PM (nonfiction)

Paulsen, G. (2005). *The quilt.* New York: Yearling. U (memory)

Polacco, P. (2001). *The keeping quilt.* New York: Aladdin Books. PM (Russian immigrant)

Ringgold, F. (2004). *Cassie's word quilt.* New York: Dragonfly. P (memory)

Root, P. (2003). *The name quilt.* New York: Farrar, Straus & Giroux. PM (memory)

Stroud, B. (2007). *The patchwork path: A quilt map to freedom.* Cambridge, MA: Candlewick Press. PM (slavery-to-freedom)

Yorinks, A. (2005). *Quilt of states: Piecing together America.* Washington, DC: National Geographic Society. MU (nonfiction)

P = primary grades (preK–2); M = middle grades (3–5); U = upper grades (6–8)

and deepen their comprehension (Mantione & Smead, 2003). They learn about the effects of colors and designs as they create quilt squares and combine them to make a quilt.

Scaffolding English Learners

English learners can participate fully in this activity because it emphasizes their artistic ability rather than their reading and writing capabilities. Students are often sought out by their classmates to make quilt squares with them, and they're just as interested as their classmates in celebrating a book they've read or a topic they've studied.

HOW TO USE THIS INSTRUCTIONAL STRATEGY

Quilt making is a whole-class activity. Teachers and students design the quilt square format together, and then students, individually or with partners, create their squares. Afterward, the teacher arranges the squares to make the quilt. This is the procedure:

1 **Design the quilt square.** Teachers and students choose a design for the quilt square that's appropriate for the story—its theme, characters, or setting. Students can choose a quilt design or create their own design that captures an important dimension of the story, and they also choose symbolic colors for each shape in the quilt square.

2 **Make the squares.** Students each make a square, adding a favorite sentence from the story or a comment about the story around the outside or in a designated section of the quilt square.

3 **Assemble the quilt.** Teachers tape the squares together and back the quilt with butcher paper, or they staple the squares side by side on a large bulletin board.

WHEN TO USE THIS INSTRUCTIONAL STRATEGY

Students make quilts as a culminating project for a literature focus unit or a thematic unit. Quilts are usually made of paper, but they can be made of cloth, too. As an end-of-the-year project or to celebrate Book Week, teachers cut out squares of light-colored cloth and have students use fabric markers to draw pictures of their favorite stories and add the titles and authors. Then teachers or other adults sew the squares together, add a border, and complete the quilt.

REFERENCES

Cobb, M. (1995). *The quilt-block history of pioneer days: With projects kids can make.* Brookfield, CT: Millbrook Press.

Hale, S. (2007). *Princess Academy.* New York: Bloomsbury.

Kirby, S. (2000). *Ellen's story.* New York: Aladdin Books.

Kirby, S. (2001). *Daniel's story.* New York: Aladdin Books.

Mantione, R. A., & Smead, S. (2003). *Weaving through words: Using the arts to teach reading comprehension strategies.* Newark, DE: International Reading Association.

Tompkins, G. E. (2013). *Language arts: Patterns of practice* (8th ed.). Boston: Allyn & Bacon/Pearson.

35 RAFT

Instructional Focus

☐ Oral Language	☑ Comprehension	
☐ Phonemic Awareness/Phonics	☑ Writing	
☐ Fluency	☐ Spelling	
☐ Vocabulary	☑ Content Areas	

Grade Levels

☐ PreK–Grade 2
☑ Grades 3–5
☑ Grades 6–8
☐ English Learners

Teachers use RAFT to create projects and other assignments to enhance students' comprehension of novels they're reading and information they're learning in thematic units (Buehl, 2008; Holston & Santa, 1985). RAFT is an acronym for *role*, *audience*, *format*, and *topic*, and teachers consider these four dimensions as they design projects:

Role of the Writer. Writers assume the role of a person or the voice of a group of people for this project. Sometimes students take on the role of a book character, historical figure, or contemporary personality, such as Oprah, but at other times, they remain themselves.

Audience. The audience is the person or people who will read or view the project; they may include students, teachers, parents, or community members, as well as simulated audiences, such as book characters and historical personalities.

Format. The format is the genre or activity that students create; it might be a letter, brochure, cartoon, journal, poster, essay, newspaper article, speech, or digital scrapbook.

Topic. The topic is the subject of the project; it may be an issue related to the text, an essential question, or something of personal interest.

When students develop projects, they process ideas and information in different ways as they assume varied viewpoints, and complete projects directed to specific audiences.

WHY USE THIS INSTRUCTIONAL STRATEGY

RAFT is an innovative way to design oral, written, and visual projects and incorporate a variety of genres and digital resources as part of literature focus units and thematic units. Students'

COMMON CORE STATE STANDARDS FOR ENGLISH LANGUAGE ARTS: *RAFT*

This instructional strategy supports these Common Core State Standards for Writing:

- Students write arguments, informative/explanatory texts, narratives, and opinion pieces.
- Students use technology to produce and publish their writing.
- Students conduct research projects to answer questions.

Students apply what they're learning about literature or content-area topics as they develop RAFT projects.

thinking is imaginative and interpretive; in contrast, their comprehension tends to be more literal when they do more traditional assignments, such as writing answers to questions.

HOW TO USE THIS INSTRUCTIONAL STRATEGY

Teachers follow these steps to use RAFT after reading a book or studying a topic during a thematic unit:

1 **Establish the purpose.** Teachers reflect on what they want students to learn through this activity and consider how it can enhance students' comprehension of a book they're reading or a social studies or science topic they're learning.

2 **Prepare a RAFT chart.** Teachers prepare a RAFT chart of possible projects by brainstorming roles, choosing audiences, identifying genres and other formats for projects, and listing topics.

3 **Read the book or study the topic.** Students read and discuss a novel or learn about a topic before they develop RAFT projects.

4 **Choose projects.** Sometimes teachers assign the same project for all students, but at other times, they vary the assignment for small groups or let students choose a project from the RAFT chart.

5 **Create projects.** Students create their projects using the writing process and get feedback from the teacher as they work.

6 **Share completed projects.** Students share their projects with small groups or the whole class and other appropriate audiences.

WHEN TO USE THIS INSTRUCTIONAL STRATEGY

RAFT is usually an after-reading activity because students develop projects after reading and discussing a novel or after studying a social studies or science topic, but it can also be used in preparation for grand conversations (see p. 45) or literature circle discussions. In addition, many teachers use RAFT as a prewriting activity to help students understand the relationships among topics, genres, and authors.

Differentiating Instruction

RAFT is an effective way to differentiate instruction by providing tiered activities; projects on the same text or topic can be adjusted according to students' achievement levels, English proficiency, and interests. For example, a seventh grade teacher developed the chart on RAFT ideas on page 108 for the Newbery Honor book *The Wednesday Wars* (Schmidt, 2007); this coming-of-age novel chronicles the everyday trials of Holling Hoodhood, who's at odds with his seventh grade English teacher, Mrs. Baker.

RAFT Ideas Chart			
Role	Audience	Format	Topic
Holling and William Shakespeare	Our class	Interview	Explain "To thine own self be true" and other life lessons.
Mrs. Baker	Her son, a U.S. soldier in Vietnam	Letter	Tell why you took such an interest in Holling.
You	Our class	Poster	Describe the cultural and political uproar of the 1960s.
You	Newbery Award Committee	Persuasive essay	Present reasons why this book should win the Newbery Award.
Bullies	Students at Camillo Jr. High	Speech	Research bullying, and explain how to deal with bullies.
Mai Thi (Holling's classmate)	Our class	Digital scrapbook	Share information about Vietnam and the war's effect on you and your home country.
Holling	Mrs. Baker	Letter, written when Holling is 30 years old	Explain how you've followed Mrs. Baker's advice: "Learn everything you can—everything. And then use all that you have learned to be a wise and good man."

REFERENCES

Buehl, D. (2008). *Classroom strategies for interactive learning* (3rd ed.). Newark, DE: International Reading Association.

Holston, V., & Santa, C. (1985). RAFT: A method of writing across the curriculum that works. *Journal of Reading, 28,* 456–457.

Schmidt, G. D. (2007). *The Wednesday wars.* New York: Clarion Books.

36 Readers Theatre

Instructional Focus

- ☐ Oral Language
- ☐ Phonemic Awareness/Phonics
- ☑ Fluency
- ☐ Vocabulary

- ☑ Comprehension
- ☐ Writing
- ☐ Spelling
- ☐ Content Areas

Grade Levels

- ☑ PreK–Grade 2
- ☑ Grades 3–5
- ☐ Grades 6–8
- ☑ English Learners

Readers theatre is a dramatic performance of a script by a group of readers (Black & Stave, 2007). Students each assume a part, rehearse by reading and rereading their character's lines in the script, and then do a performance for their classmates. What's valuable is that students interpret the story with their voices, without using much action. They may stand or sit, but they must carry the whole communication of the plot, characterization, mood, and theme through their voices, gestures, and facial expressions. Readers theatre avoids many of the restrictions inherent in theatrical productions: Students don't memorize their parts; elaborate props, costumes, and backdrops aren't needed; and long, tedious hours aren't spent rehearsing.

Students can read scripts in trade books and textbooks, or they can create their own scripts. The Booklist on page 110 presents 10 books of narrative and nonfiction scripts for readers theatre.

WHY USE THIS INSTRUCTIONAL STRATEGY

There are many reasons to recommend readers theatre. Students have opportunities to enjoy reading good literature, and through this strategy they engage with text, interpret characters, and bring the text to life (Keehn, Martinez, & Roser, 2005; Larkin, 2001; Worthy & Prater, 2002). Moreover, students develop reading fluency as they read and reread their lines (Fountas & Pinnell, 2001; Young & Rasinski, 2009).

Scaffolding English Learners

Readers theatre is an especially effective for strategy for English learners and other students who aren't fluent readers. They gain valuable oral reading practice in a relaxed, small-group setting; they practice reading high-frequency words, increase their reading speed, learn how to phrase and chunk words in sentences, and read with more expression.

COMMON CORE STATE STANDARDS FOR ENGLISH LANGUAGE ARTS: *READERS THEATRE*

This instructional strategy supports these Common Core State Standards for Reading: Literature and Reading: Foundational Skills:

- Students demonstrate how a speaker's viewpoint influences how events are described.
- Students apply grade-level phonics and word-analysis skills.
- Students read with sufficient fluency to support comprehension.

Students become more fluent readers through readers theatre activities.

BOOKLIST

Readers Theatre Scripts

Barchers, S. I. (1997). *50 fabulous fables: Beginning readers theatre*. Portsmouth, NH: Teacher Ideas Press. P

Barchers, S. I., & Pfeffinger, C. R. (2006). *More readers theatre for beginning readers*. Portsmouth, NH: Teacher Ideas Press. P

Fredericks, A. D. (2007). *Nonfiction readers theatre for beginning readers*. Portsmouth, NH: Teacher Ideas Press. P

Laughlin, M. K., Black, P. T., & Loberg, M. K. (1991). *Social studies readers theatre for children: Scripts and script development*. Portsmouth, NH: Teacher Ideas Press. PM

Martin, J. M. (2002). *12 fabulously funny fairy tale plays*. New York: Scholastic. M

Pugliano-Martin, C. (1999). *25 just-right plays for emergent readers*. New York: Scholastic. PM

Shepard, A. (2005). *Stories on stage: Children's plays for reader's theater with 15 play scripts from 15 authors*. Olympia, WA: Shepard. M

Wolf, J. M. (2002). *Cinderella outgrows the glass slipper and other zany fractured fairy tale plays*. New York: Scholastic. M

Wolfman, J. (2004). *How and why stories for readers theatre*. Portsmouth, NH: Teacher Ideas Press. M

Worthy, J. (2008). *Readers theatre for building fluency: Strategies and scripts for making the most of this highly effective, motivating, and research-based approach to oral reading*. New York: Scholastic. PM

P = primary grades (preK–2); M = middle grades (3–5)

HOW TO USE THIS INSTRUCTIONAL STRATEGY

Teachers work with small groups or the whole class, depending on the number of parts in the script, and they follow this procedure:

1 **Select a script.** Students and the teacher select a script and then read and discuss it as they would any other story. Next, students volunteer to read each part.

2 **Rehearse the production.** Students decide how to use their voices, gestures, and facial expressions to interpret the characters they're reading. They read the script several times, striving for accurate pronunciation, voice projection, and appropriate inflections. Less rehearsal is required for an informal, in-class presentation than for a more formal production; nevertheless, interpretations should always be developed as fully as possible.

3 **Stage the production.** Readers theatre can be presented on a stage or in the front of the classroom. Students stand or sit in a row and read their lines in the script. They stay in position through the production or enter and leave according to the characters' appearances "onstage." If readers are sitting, they may stand to read their lines; if they're standing, they may step forward to read. The emphasis isn't on production quality; rather, it's on the interpretive quality of the readers' voices and expressions. Costumes and props are unnecessary; however, adding a few small props can enhance interest and enjoyment as long as they don't interfere with the interpretive quality of the reading.

GO DIGITAL

Podcasts

Teachers create podcasts of students' readers theatre productions and then post them on the classroom website for parents and students to enjoy. They use external computer microphones and Audacity recording software to record the scripted reading; then they upload and edit the files before posting them online. Vasinda and McLeod (2011) researched the effectiveness of creating podcasts of students' readers theatre productions, and they found that technology does enhance this instructional strategy.

WHEN TO USE THIS INSTRUCTIONAL STRATEGY

Students can create their own readers theatre scripts from stories they've read and about topics related to thematic units (Flynn, 2007). When students are creating a script from

The First Page of "The Elves and the Shoemaker"

Characters

Narrator 1	Shoemaker	Lady 1	Elf 1
Narrator 2	Wife	Lady 2	Elf 2
Narrator 3	Man		Elf 3

Narrator 1: Once upon a time there was a good shoemaker and his wife, but they were very poor. The shoemaker had only one piece of leather to make into shoes.

Shoemaker: Tonight I will cut my last piece of leather to make a pair of shoes. I will make a pair of shiny black shoes for a man. Then I will sew the shoes in the morning.

Narrator 2: The next morning the shoemaker went to his work table but he couldn't believe what he saw.

Shoemaker: I can't believe my eyes. What a fine pair of shiny new shoes!

Wife: What did you say?

Shoemaker: Come and see what I see.

Wife: Who made these shiny new shoes?

Shoemaker: I do not know. It is like magic!

Narrator 3: At that very moment, a man came into the shoemaker's shop.

Man: Those shoes look just right for me. May I try them on?

Narrator 1: The man put on the shoes and they were just right for him.

Man: How much do these shiny new shoes cost?

Shoemaker: They cost one gold coin.

Man: Because I like them so much, I will give you two gold coins for the shoes.

Shoemaker: We are so fortunate! Now we can buy leather to make two more pairs of shoes.

a story, it's important to choose a story with a lot of conversations; any parts that don't include dialogue become narrator parts. Depending on the number of narrator parts, one to four students can share the narrator duties. Teachers often make photocopies of the book for students to mark up or highlight as they develop the script. Sometimes students simply use their marked-up copies as the finished script, and at other times, teachers retype the script, leaving out unnecessary parts and using the script format. The first page of a second grade class's script for "The Elves and the Shoemaker" is shown on above.

REFERENCES

Black, A., & Stave, A. M. (2007). *A comprehensive guide to readers theatre: Enhancing fluency and comprehension in middle school and beyond.* Newark, DE: International Reading Association.

Flynn, R. M. (2007). *Dramatizing the content with curriculum-based readers theatre, grades 6–12.* Newark, DE: International Reading Association.

Fountas, I. C., & Pinnell, G. S. (2001). *Guiding readers and writers, grades 3–6.* Portsmouth, NH: Heinemann.

Keehn, S., Martinez, M. G., & Roser, N. L. (2005). Exploring character through readers theatre. In N. L. Roser & M. G. Martinez (Eds.), *What a character! Character study as a guide to literary meaning making in grades K–8* (pp. 96–110). Newark, DE: International Reading Association.

Larkin, B. R. (2001). "Can we act it out?" *The Reading Teacher, 54,* 478–481.

Vasinda, S., & McLeod, J. (2011). Extending readers theatre: A powerful and purposeful match with podcasting. *The Reading Teacher, 64,* 486–497.

Worthy, J., & Prater, K. (2002). "I thought about it all night": Readers theatre for reading fluency and motivation. *The Reading Teacher, 56,* 294–297.

Young, C., & Rasinski, T. (2009). Implementing readers theatre as an approach to classroom fluency instruction. *The Reading Teacher, 63,* 4–13.

37 Reading Logs

Instructional Focus

☐ Oral Language	☑ Comprehension	
☐ Phonemic Awareness/Phonics	☑ Writing	
☐ Fluency	☐ Spelling	
☐ Vocabulary	☐ Content Areas	

Grade Levels

- ☑ PreK–Grade 2
- ☑ Grades 3–5
- ☑ Grades 6–8
- ☐ English Learners

Reading logs are journals in which students write their reactions and opinions about books they're reading or listening to the teacher read aloud. Through their reading log entries, students clarify misunderstandings, explore ideas, and deepen their comprehension (Barone, 1990; Hancock, 2008). They also add lists of words from the word wall (see p. 156), diagrams about story elements, and information about authors and genres (Tompkins, 2012). For a chapter book, students write after reading every chapter or two, and they often write single entries after reading picture books or short stories. Often students write a series of entries about a collection of books written by the same author, such as books by Eric Carle or Chris Van Allsburg, or about versions of the same folktale or fairy tale.

Sometimes students choose what they'll write about in reading log entries, and at other times, they respond to questions or prompts that teachers have prepared. Both student-choice and teacher-directed entries are useful: When students choose their own topics, they delve into their own ideas and questions, sharing what's important to them, and when teachers prepare prompts, they direct students' thinking to topics and questions that students might otherwise miss. When teachers know their students well and are familiar with the books students are reading, they choose the best mix of student-choice and teacher-directed entries.

WHY USE THIS INSTRUCTIONAL STRATEGY

The primary purpose of reading logs is for students to think about the book they're reading and deepen their understanding of the story. Students use writing as a tool for learning, and an additional benefit is that they develop writing fluency as they make their entries.

COMMON CORE STATE STANDARDS FOR ENGLISH LANGUAGE ARTS: *READING LOGS*

This instructional strategy supports these Common Core State Standards for Reading: Literature and Writing:

- Students comprehend grade-appropriate stories.
- Students examine the theme and other elements of story structure.
- Students compare characters, settings, and events in a story.

Students build and integrate knowledge as they make entries in reading logs.

HOW TO USE THIS INSTRUCTIONAL STRATEGY

Students write independently in reading logs. Sometimes all students in the class write at the same time, and at other times, students choose their own times to write. Teachers follow this procedure:

1 **Prepare the reading logs.** Students make reading logs by stapling paper into booklets, and they write the title of the book on the cover.

2 **Write entries.** Students write their reactions and reflections about the book or chapter. Sometimes they choose their own topics, and at other times, teachers assign topics and pose questions. In their entries, students often summarize events and relate the book to their own lives, the world around them, or other literature they've read. They also list interesting or unfamiliar words, jot down quotable quotes, and take notes about characters, plot, or other story elements.

3 **Monitor students' entries.** Teachers check that students have completed the entries. They also write comments back to students about their interpretations and reflections. Because students' writing in reading logs is informal, teachers don't expect them to spell every word correctly, but they do expect them to correctly spell characters' names, high-frequency words, and other words they've been taught to spell.

WHEN TO USE THIS INSTRUCTIONAL STRATEGY

Students at all grade levels can write and draw reading log entries to help them understand stories they're reading and listening to read aloud during literature focus units and literature circles (Daniels, 2001). The box below shows a page from a third grader's reading log. In this entry, the student has responded to John Steptoe's *The Story of Jumping Mouse* (1989), a Native American legend about how a generous mouse was transformed into an eagle.

A Third Grader's Reading Log Entry

The Story Of the Jumping Mouse
by John Steptoe

This story shows that it never hurts to help. And I think that the pictures are really good. My favorite part is when the mouse turned into an eagle. The mouse was the most generous.

As a sixth grade class read *The Giver* (Lowry, 2006), a Newbery Award–winning story of a not-so-perfect society, students discussed each chapter and brainstormed several possible chapter titles. Then they wrote entries in their reading logs and labeled each chapter with the number and the title they decided was most appropriate. The following three reading log entries show how a sixth grader grappled with the idea of "release": After reading and discussing Chapter 18, the student doesn't understand that "release" means "killing," but he grasps the awful meaning of the word as he reads Chapter 19.

Chapter 18: "Release"

I think release is very rude. People have a right to live where they want to. Just because they're different they have to go somewhere else. I think release is when you have to go and live elsewhere. If you're released you can't come back to the community.

Chapter 19: "Release–The Truth"

It is so mean to kill people that didn't do anything bad. They kill perfectly innocent people. Everyone has a right to live. The shot is even worse to give them. They should be able to die on their own. If I were Jonas I would probably go insane. The people who kill the people that are to be released don't know what they're doing.

Chapter 20: "Mortified"

I don't think that Jonas is going to be able to go home and face his father. What can he do? Now that he knows what release is he will probably stay with The Giver for the rest of his life until he is released.

GO DIGITAL

Blogs

Instead of responding to literature in reading logs, students can post blogs about books they're reading on a kid-friendly gated site that controls who can post, comment on, and view blogs, and classmates read and respond to their entries. Classmates' comments are essential because they stimulate discussion, expand topics, and keep students thinking and writing. Teachers ensure that all students are respected because they set ground rules and monitor students' comments before they're published.

REFERENCES

Barone, D. (1990). The written responses of young children: Beyond comprehension to story understanding. *The New Advocate, 3,* 49–56.

Daniels, H. (2001). *Literature circles: Voice and choice in book clubs and reading groups.* York, ME: Stenhouse.

Hancock, M. R. (2008). *A celebration of literature and response: Children, books, and teachers in K–8 classrooms* (3rd ed.). Upper Saddle River, NJ: Merrill/Prentice Hall.

Lowry, L. (2006). *The giver.* New York: Delacorte.

Steptoe, J. (1989). *The story of Jumping Mouse.* New York: Harper Trophy.

Tompkins, G. E. (2012). *Teaching writing: Balancing process and product* (6th ed.). Boston: Allyn & Bacon/Pearson.

38 Revising Groups

Instructional Focus

- ☐ Oral Language
- ☐ Phonemic Awareness/Phonics
- ☐ Fluency
- ☐ Vocabulary

- ☐ Comprehension
- ☑ Writing
- ☐ Spelling
- ☐ Content Areas

Grade Levels

- ☐ PreK–Grade 2
- ☑ Grades 3–5
- ☑ Grades 6–8
- ☐ English Learners

During the revising stage of the writing process, students meet in groups to share their rough drafts and get feedback on how well they're communicating (Tompkins, 2012). Revising group members are good critics: They offer compliments about things writers have done well and make suggestions for improvement (Lane, 1999). They make comments abut these topics and other aspects of the writer's craft that they've learned about:

leads	word choice	voice
dialogue	sentences	rhyme
endings	character development	sequence
description	point of view	flashbacks
ideas	organization	alliterations

These topics are used for both compliments and suggestions. When students are offering a compliment, they might say, "I liked your lead. It grabbed me and made me keep listening"; and when they're making a suggestion, they say, "I wonder if you could start with a question to make your lead more interesting. Maybe you could say, 'Have you ever ridden in a police car? Well, that's what happened to me!'"

Teaching students how to share their rough drafts in a revising group and offer constructive feedback isn't easy. When teachers introduce revision, they model appropriate responses because students may not know how to offer specific and meaningful comments tactfully. Teachers and students can brainstorm a list of appropriate compliments and suggestions and post it in the classroom to refer to. Comments should usually begin with "I," not "you." Notice the difference in tone in these two sentence stems: "I wonder if . . . " versus "You need to . . . " Here are some ways to begin compliments:

I like the part where . . .
I learned how . . .

COMMON CORE STATE STANDARDS FOR ENGLISH LANGUAGE ARTS: *REVISING GROUPS*

This instructional strategy supports these Common Core State Standards for Writing:

- Students write a variety of compositions, including narratives, informative texts, and opinion pieces.
- Students revise their writing with guidance and support from teachers.

Students participate in revising groups with classmates and the teacher to improve the effectiveness of their writing.

I like the way you described . . .

I like how you organized the information because . . .

Students also offer suggestions about how classmates can revise their writing. It's important that students phrase what they say in helpful ways. Here are some ways to begin suggestions:

I got confused in the part about . . .

I wonder if you need a closing . . .

I'd like you to add more about . . .

I wonder if these paragraphs are in the right order . . .

I think you might want to combine these sentences . . .

Student-writers also ask classmates for help with specific problems they've identified. Looking to classmates for feedback is a big step in learning to revise. Here are some questions writers can ask:

What do you want to know more about?

Is there a part that I should throw away?

What details can I add?

What do you think is the best part of my writing?

Are there some words I need to change?

Revising groups work effectively once students understand how to support and help their classmates by offering compliments, making suggestions, and asking questions.

WHY USE THIS INSTRUCTIONAL STRATEGY

Revising is the most difficult part of the writing process because it's hard for students to stand back and evaluate their writing objectively in order to make changes to communicate more effectively. As students participate in revising groups, they learn how to accept compliments and suggestions and to provide useful feedback to classmates.

HOW TO USE THIS INSTRUCTIONAL STRATEGY

Teachers teach students how to use this instructional strategy so that they can then work in small groups to get ideas for revising their writing. Small groups work most effectively with four students in a group. Here is the procedure:

1 **Read drafts aloud.** Students take turns reading their rough drafts aloud to the group. Everyone listens politely, thinking about compliments and suggestions they'll make after the writer finishes reading. Only the writer looks at the composition because when classmates look at it, they quickly notice and comment on mechanical errors, even though the emphasis during revision is on content. Listening to the writing read aloud keeps the focus on content.

2 **Offer compliments.** After listening to the rough draft read aloud, classmates in the revising group tell the writer what they liked about the composition. These positive comments should be specific, focusing on strengths, rather than the often-heard "I liked it" or "It was good"; even though these are positive comments, they don't provide effective feedback.

3 **Ask clarifying questions.** After a round of positive comments, writers ask for assistance with trouble spots they identified earlier when rereading their writing, or they may ask questions that reflect more general concerns about how well they're communicating.

4 **Offer other revision suggestions.** Members of the revising group ask questions about things that were unclear to them and make suggestions about how to revise the rough draft.

5 **Repeat the process.** Members of the revising group repeat the process so that all students can share their rough drafts. The first four steps are repeated for each student's composition.

6 **Make plans for revision.** At the end of the revising group session, students each make a commitment to revise their writing based on the comments and suggestions of the group members. The final decisions on what to revise always rest with the writers themselves, but with the understanding that their rough drafts aren't perfect comes the realization that some revision will be necessary. When students verbalize their planned revisions, they're more likely to complete the revision stage.

WHEN TO USE THIS INSTRUCTIONAL STRATEGY

Students meet in revising groups whenever they're using the writing process. Once they've written a rough draft, students are ready to share their writing and get some feedback from classmates. They often meet with the same revising group throughout the school year, or students can form groups when they're ready to get feedback about their rough drafts. When students are working together on a writing project, such as writing a sequel after reading a book during a literature focus unit or writing reports on desert plants and animals as part of a thematic unit on the desert, many students will be ready to meet in revising groups at approximately the same time, so they can meet in groups according to established groups in the classroom. In contrast, during writing workshop, students work on writing projects at their own speed, and students need to meet in revising groups at different times. Many teachers have students sign up on the whiteboard; this way, whenever four students are ready, they form a group. Both established and spontaneously formed groups can be effective. What matters most is that students get feedback about their writing when they need it.

REFERENCES

Lane, B. (1999). *Reviser's toolbox*. Shoreham, VT: Discover Writing Press.

Tompkins, G. E. (2012). *Teaching writing: Balancing process and product* (6th ed.). Boston: Allyn & Bacon/Pearson.

39 Rubrics

. . . .

Instructional Focus		Grade Levels
☑ Oral Language	☐ Comprehension	☐ PreK–Grade 2
☐ Phonemic Awareness/Phonics	☑ Writing	☑ Grades 3–5
☐ Fluency	☐ Spelling	☑ Grades 6–8
☐ Vocabulary	☑ Content Areas	☐ English Learners

Rubrics are scoring guides that teachers use to assess students' achievement on writing and other types of projects (Farr & Tone, 1994). These guides usually have 4, 5, or 6 levels, ranging from high to low, and assessment criteria are described at each level. Students receive a copy of the rubric as they begin a project so that they understand what's expected and how they'll be assessed. Depending on the rubric's intricacy, teachers mark the assessment criteria either while they're reading or examining the project or immediately afterward, and then they determine the overall score.

The assessment criteria in rubrics vary. The requirements in rubrics for oral presentations often focus on eye contact, composure, and the quality of the content presented; and the criteria in rubrics for museum projects describe the quality of artifacts and curator's notes, accuracy and completeness of information that's presented, Standard English conventions used in written text, and bibliographic resources. Criteria in general writing rubrics address the qualities of effective writing, such as ideas, organization, word choice, and mechanics. Other rubrics are genre specific, and deal with genre characteristics; teachers often use these rubrics to assess stories, reports, and autobiographies. No matter which assessment criteria are used, the same criteria are addressed at each achievement level. If a criterion addresses sentence fluency, for example, descriptors about sentence fluency are included at each level; the statement "contains short, choppy sentences" might be used at the lowest level and "uses sentences that vary in length and style" at the highest level. Each level represents a one-step improvement in students' application of that criterion. A fifth grade writing rubric is shown on page 120.

Rubrics can be constructed with any number of levels, but it's easier to show growth when a rubric has more levels. Much more improvement is needed for students to move from one level to the next if the rubric has 4 levels than if it has 6 levels. A rubric with 10 levels would be even more sensitive, but rubrics with many levels are harder to construct and more time-consuming to use. Researchers generally recommend that teachers use rubrics

COMMON CORE STATE STANDARDS FOR ENGLISH LANGUAGE ARTS: *RUBRICS*

This instructional strategy supports these Common Core State Standards for Reading: Informational Text, Writing, and Language:

- Students integrate information in varied media and formats.
- Students use academic vocabulary appropriately.
- Students produce clear and coherent oral and written presentations.
- Students demonstrate command of Standard English grammar, spelling, and conventions.

Students use rubrics to improve the quality of their projects.

with either 4 or 6 levels so that there's no middle score—each level is either above or below the middle—because teachers are inclined to score students at the middle level, when there is one.

Rubrics are often used for determining proficiency levels and assigning grades. The level that's above the midpoint is usually designated as "proficient," "competent," or "passing"—that's a 3 on a 4-point rubric and a 4 on a 5- or 6-point rubric. The levels on a 6-point rubric can be described this way:

1 = minimal level	4 = proficient level
2 = beginning or limited level	5 = commendable level
3 = developing level	6 = exceptional level

Teachers also equate levels to letter grades.

Fifth Grade Writing Rubric	
5	**EXCEPTIONAL ACHIEVEMENT**
	• Creative and original • Clear organization • Precise word choice and figurative language • Sophisticated sentences • Essentially free of mechanical errors
4	**GOOD ACHIEVEMENT**
	• Some creativity, but more predictable than an exceptional paper • Definite organization • Good word choice, but no figurative language • Varied sentences • Only a few mechanical errors
3	**NEARLY ADEQUATE ACHIEVEMENT**
	• Predictable paper • Some organization • Adequate word choice • Little variety of sentences, and some run-on sentences • Some mechanical errors
2	**LIMITED ACHIEVEMENT**
	• Brief and superficial • Lacks organization • Imprecise language • Incomplete and run-on sentences • Many mechanical errors
1	**MINIMAL ACHIEVEMENT**
	• No ideas communicated • No organization • Inadequate word choice • Sentence fragments • Overwhelming mechanical errors

WHY USE THIS INSTRUCTIONAL STRATEGY

These scoring guides help students become better writers, give more effective oral performances, or create more thoughtful projects, because they lay out the qualities that constitute excellence and clarify teachers' expectations so students understand how the assignment will be assessed. Students, too, can use rubrics to improve the quality of their work. For example, writers examine their rough drafts and decide how to revise their writing to make it more effective based on the rubric's criteria. In addition, Vicki Spandel (2005) claims that rubrics are time savers: She says that using rubrics drastically cuts the time it takes to read and respond to students' writing because the criteria on the rubric guide the assessment and reduce the need to write lengthy comments back to students.

HOW TO USE THIS INSTRUCTIONAL STRATEGY

Teachers introduce the rubric to the class, and then students refer to it as they create products and develop presentations. Later, teachers use the rubric to assess students' work. They follow this procedure:

1 **Choose a rubric.** Teachers choose a rubric that's appropriate to the project or create one that reflects the assignment.

2 **Introduce the rubric.** Teachers distribute copies of the rubric to students and talk about the criteria used at each level, focusing on the requirements at the proficiency level.

3 **Self-assess progress.** Students use the rubric to self-assess their progress at a midway point or their writing during the revising stage. They highlight phrases in the rubric or check off items that best describe the quality of their work. Then they determine which level has the most highlighted words or checkmarks; that level is the overall score, and students circle it.

4 **Assess students' projects.** Teachers assess students' oral or written projects by highlighting phrases in the rubric or checking off items that best describe the quality of the work. They assign the overall score by determining which level has the most highlighted words or checkmarks and circle it.

5 **Conference with students.** Teachers talk with students about the assessment, identifying strengths and weaknesses. Then students set goals for the next project.

WHEN TO USE THIS INSTRUCTIONAL STRATEGY

Teachers use rubrics to assess the quality of projects students develop individually, with partners, and in small groups. They assess the compositions students write during writing workshop and evaluate students' oral performances and written products during literature focus units and thematic units. Many commercially prepared rubrics are currently available: State departments of education post rubrics for mandated writing tests on their websites, and school districts hire teams of teachers or consultants to develop writing rubrics for each grade level. Spandel (2005) has rubrics that assess the six traits of writing. Other rubrics are provided with reading textbook programs, in professional books for teachers, and on the Internet.

Even though commercially prepared rubrics are convenient, they may not be appropriate for some groups of students or for specific projects: They may have only 4 levels when 6 would be better, or they may have been developed for a different grade level. Or, they may have been written for teachers, not in kid-friendly language. Because of these limitations, teachers often decide to develop their own rubrics or adapt commercial rubrics to meet their needs.

REFERENCES

Farr, R., & Tone, B. (1994). *Portfolio and performance assessment: Helping students evaluate their progress as readers and writers*. Fort Worth, TX: Harcourt Brace.

Spandel, V. (2005). *Creating writers: Through 6-trait writing assessment and instruction* (4th ed.). Boston: Allyn & Bacon.

40 Shared Reading

Instructional Focus		Grade Levels
☐ Oral Language	☑ Comprehension	☑ PreK–Grade 2
☐ Phonemic Awareness/Phonics	☐ Writing	☐ Grades 3–5
☑ Fluency	☐ Spelling	☐ Grades 6–8
☐ Vocabulary	☐ Content Areas	☑ English Learners

Teachers use shared reading to read authentic literature—stories, nonfiction books, and poems—with children who could not read those books independently (Holdaway, 1979). Teachers read the book aloud, modeling fluent reading, and then they read the book again and again over a period of 3 to 5 days and use it for reading instruction. The focus during the first reading is children's enjoyment. During the next couple of readings, teachers draw children's attention to concepts about print, comprehension, and interesting language. Finally, they move to decoding and focus children's attention on particular words during the last reading or two.

Children are actively involved in shared reading. Teachers encourage them to make predictions and to chime in on repeated words and phrases. Individual children or small groups take turns reading brief parts once they begin to recognize words and phrases. Children examine interesting features that they notice in the book—punctuation marks, illustrations, tables of contents, for example—and teachers point out others. They also talk about the book, both while they're reading and afterward. Shared reading builds on children's experience listening to their parents read bedtime stories (Fisher & Medvic, 2000).

WHY USE THIS INSTRUCTIONAL STRATEGY

There are many reasons to recommend shared reading. Teachers use this instructional strategy to read authentic literature that children can't read themselves. They serve as models of fluent reading, and they take advantage of opportunities to point out concepts of print and teach word-recognition skills (Fountas & Pinnell, 1996). Children develop their reading fluency and knowledge of high-frequency words; and shared reading is a good way to teach comprehension strategies because students can focus on using the strategy without trying to decode the text. Shared reading often motivates children to reread the books they've listened to the teacher read and to read other books on their own. In addition, Allen (2002) claims that shared reading can even change the classroom atmosphere.

COMMON CORE STATE STANDARDS FOR ENGLISH LANGUAGE ARTS: *SHARED READING*

This instructional strategy supports these Common Core State Standards for Reading: Foundational Skills:

- Students demonstrate understanding of organization and basic features of print.
- Students identify common high-frequency words in big books.
- Students read with purpose and understanding.

Students learn many concepts about how written language works through shared reading.

Scaffolding English Learners

Teachers share grade-appropriate books with English learners that they couldn't read on their own, and during shared reading, English learners have many opportunities to listen to a fluent English speaker reading aloud while they follow along, looking at the words. They're encouraged to join in and read familiar words whenever they can, but there isn't any pressure to perform.

HOW TO USE THIS INSTRUCTIONAL STRATEGY

Teachers use shared reading with both the whole class and small groups of students, and they follow this procedure:

1 **Introduce the text.** Teachers talk about the book or other text by activating or building background knowledge on topics related to the book, reading the title and the author's name aloud, and examining the cover illustration or doing a picture walk through the book.

2 **Read the text aloud.** Teachers read the story aloud to students, using a pointer (a dowel rod with a pencil eraser on the end) to track as they read. They invite students to be actively involved by making predictions and joining in the reading, especially if the story is repetitive.

3 **Have a grand conversation (see p. 45).** Teachers invite students to talk about the story, ask questions, and share their responses.

4 **Reread the story.** Students take turns using the pointer to track the reading and turning pages. Teachers invite students to join in reading familiar and predictable words. Also, they take opportunities to teach and use graphophonic cues and reading strategies while reading. Teachers vary the support that they provide, depending on students' reading expertise.

5 **Continue the process.** Teachers continue to reread the story with students over a period of several days, again having students turn pages and take turns using the pointer to track the text while reading. They encourage students who can read the text to read along with them.

6 **Read independently.** After students become familiar with the text, teachers distribute individual copies of the book or other text for students to read independently and use for a variety of activities.

WHEN TO USE THIS INSTRUCTIONAL STRATEGY

Shared reading is a step between reading aloud and children doing their own reading (Parkes, 2000). Teachers use this instructional strategy to read books that students can't read on their own during literature focus units, literature circles, and thematic units. When doing shared reading with young children, teachers use enlarged texts, including big books, poems written on charts, Language Experience stories (see p. 64), and interactive writing charts (see p. 56), so that children can see the text and read along. For older students, teachers use shared reading techniques to read books that students could not read themselves (Allen, 2002). Students each have a copy of the text—a novel, content-area textbook, or other book—and the teacher and students read together. The teacher or another fluent reader reads aloud while other students follow along in the text, reading to themselves.

REFERENCES

Allen, J. (2002). *On the same page: Shared reading beyond the primary grades.* York, ME: Stenhouse.

Fisher, B., & Medvic, E. F. (2000). *Perspectives on shared reading: Planning and practice.* Portsmouth, NH: Heinemann.

Fountas, I. C., & Pinnell, G. S. (1996). *Guided reading: Good first teaching for all children.* Portsmouth, NH: Heinemann.

Holdaway, D. (1979). *Foundations of literacy.* Auckland, NZ: Ashton Scholastic.

Parkes, B. (2000). *Read it again! Revisiting shared reading.* York, ME: Stenhouse.

41 Sketch-to-Stretch

Instructional Focus		Grade Levels
☐ Oral Language	☑ Comprehension	☐ PreK–Grade 2
☐ Phonemic Awareness/Phonics	☐ Writing	☑ Grades 3–5
☐ Fluency	☐ Spelling	☑ Grades 6–8
☐ Vocabulary	☐ Content Areas	☐ English Learners

Sketch-to-stretch is a visual activity that moves students beyond literal comprehension of a story they're reading to think more deeply about the characters, theme, and other elements of story structure and the author's craft (Harste, Short, & Burke, 1988; Short & Harste, 1996). Students work in small groups to draw pictures or diagrams to represent what the story means to them, not pictures of their favorite character or episode. In their sketches, students use lines, shapes, colors, symbols, and words to express their interpretations and feelings. Because students work in a social setting with the support of classmates, they share ideas, extend their understanding, and generate new insights (Whitin, 1994, 1996).

Students need many opportunities to experiment with this activity before they move beyond drawing pictures of the story events or characters and are able to think symbolically. It's helpful to introduce this instructional strategy through a minilesson (see p. 74) and to draw several sketches together as a class before students do their own sketches. Through this practice, students learn that there's no single correct interpretation, and teachers help students focus on the interpretation rather than on their artistic talents (Ernst, 1993). The box on the next page shows a fourth grader's sketch-to-stretch made after reading *The Ballad of Lucy Whipple* (Cushman, 1996), a story set during the California gold rush. The sketch-to-stretch emphasizes two of the themes of the book—that you make your own happiness, and that home is where you are.

WHY USE THIS INSTRUCTIONAL STRATEGY

Sketch-to-stretch is an effective tool for helping students deepen their understanding of stories they're reading. In particular, students focus on theme and on the use of symbols to represent characters and theme as they make sketch-to-stretch drawings (Dooley & Maloch, 2005). An added benefit is that through this activity, students learn that stories rarely have only one interpretation, and that by reflecting on the characters and events in a story, they can discover one or more themes.

COMMON CORE STATE STANDARDS FOR ENGLISH LANGUAGE ARTS: *SKETCH-TO-STRETCH*

This instructional strategy supports these Common Core State Standards for Reading: Literature:

- Students explain what a text quote says and draw inferences from it.
- Students apply their knowledge of the structure and craft of stories.
- Students read and comprehend grade-appropriate stories.

Students use the sketch-to-stretch instructional strategy to deepen their understanding of stories.

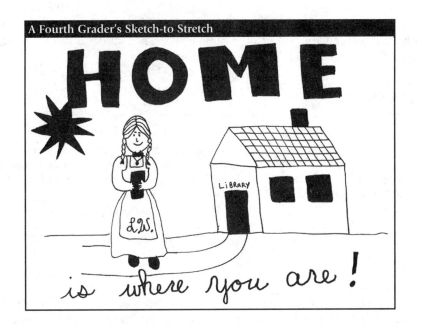

A Fourth Grader's Sketch-to Stretch

HOW TO USE THIS INSTRUCTIONAL STRATEGY

Students create sketch-to-stretch drawings individually and then share them in small groups and sometimes with the whole class. Teachers follow this procedure:

1 **Read and respond to a story.** Students read a story or several chapters of a longer book, and they respond to the story in a grand conversation (see p. 45) or in reading logs (see p. 113).

2 **Discuss the themes.** Students and the teacher talk about the themes in the story and ways to symbolize meanings. Teachers remind students that there are many ways to represent the meaning of an experience, and that students can use lines, colors, shapes, symbols, and words to visually represent what a story means to them. Students and the teacher talk about possible meanings and ways they might visually represent them.

3 **Draw the sketches.** Students work in small groups to draw sketches that reflect what the story means to them. Teachers emphasize that students should focus on their thinking about the meaning of the story, not their favorite part, and that there's no single correct interpretation. They also remind students that the artistic quality of their drawings is less important than their interpretation.

4 **Share the sketches.** Students meet in small groups to share their sketches and talk about the symbols they used. Teachers encourage classmates to study each student's sketch and tell what they think the student is trying to convey.

5 **Share some sketches.** Each group chooses one sketch from their group to share with the class.

6 **Revise sketches and make final copies.** Some students will want to revise and add to their sketches based on feedback they received and ideas from classmates. Also, students make final copies if the sketches are being used as projects.

WHEN TO USE THIS INSTRUCTIONAL STRATEGY

Students use sketch-to-stretch to deepen their comprehension whenever they're reading and discussing a story. In literature circles, for example, students create sketch-to-stretch drawings about themes and symbols that they share during group meetings (Whitin,

2002). Through this sharing, students gain insights about their classmates' thinking and clarify their own understanding. The same is true when students create and share sketch-to-stretch drawings during literature focus units.

REFERENCES

Cushman, K. (1996). *The ballad of Lucy Whipple*. New York: Clarion Books.

Dooley, C. M., & Maloch, B. (2005). Exploring characters through visual representations. In N. L. Roser & M. G. Martinez (Eds.), *What a character! Character study as a guide to literary meaning making in grades K–8* (pp. 111–123). Newark, DE: International Reading Association.

Ernst, K. (1993). *Picturing learning*. Portsmouth, NH: Heinemann.

Harste, J. C., Short, K. G., & Burke, C. (1988). *Creating classrooms for authors: The reading-writing connection*. Portsmouth, NH: Heinemann.

Short, K. G., & Harste, J. (1996). *Creating classrooms for authors and inquirers*. Portsmouth, NH: Heinemann.

Whitin, P. E. (1994). Opening potential: Visual response to literature. *Language Arts, 71*, 101–107.

Whitin, P. E. (1996). *Sketching stories, stretching minds*. Portsmouth, NH: Heinemann.

Whitin, P. E. (2002). Leading into literature circles through the sketch-to-stretch strategy. *The Reading Teacher, 55*, 444–450.

42 SQ4R Study Strategy

Instructional Focus		Grade Levels
☐ Oral Language	☑ Comprehension	☐ PreK–Grade 2
☐ Phonemic Awareness/Phonics	☐ Writing	☐ Grades 3–5
☐ Fluency	☐ Spelling	☑ Grades 6–8
☐ Vocabulary	☑ Content Areas	☐ English Learners

In the SQ4R study strategy, students use six steps—survey, question, read, recite, relate, and review—to read and remember information in content-area reading assignments (Anderson & Armbruster, 1984). The purpose of the strategy is to create a mental framework so that students get the maximum benefit from reading. The acronym was coined more than a half century ago by F. P. Robinson (1946), and it's become the most widely used study strategy. This instructional strategy is very effective when students apply it correctly, so it's important that teachers teach students how to apply the steps and provide opportunities for them to practice using the strategy correctly.

WHY USE THIS INSTRUCTIONAL STRATEGY

SQ4R is the best known study strategy, and it remains the most commonly used tool for remembering information from chapters in content-area textbooks (Daniels & Zemelman, 2004). It's effective because students do more than just read through the text; they slow down and move through a series of steps to remember the big ideas presented in the reading assignment.

HOW TO USE THIS INSTRUCTIONAL STRATEGY

Students implement this study strategy independently and use it to guide their study of content-area textbooks. Teachers direct students to follow this procedure:

1 **Survey.** Students survey or preview the reading assignment, noting headings and skimming, or rapidly reading, the introduction and the summary. They note the main ideas that are presented to activate prior knowledge and to organize what they'll read.

2 **Question.** Students turn each heading into a question before reading the section. Reading to find the answer to the question gives students a purpose for reading.

COMMON CORE STATE STANDARDS FOR ENGLISH LANGUAGE ARTS: *SQ4R*

This instructional strategy supports these Common Core State Standards for Reading: Informational Text:

- Students identify main ideas in a text.
- Students cite textual evidence to support their understanding.
- Students analyze the relationship between individuals, events, and ideas in a text.

Students use SQ4R to study content-area textbook chapters and comprehend other nonfiction texts.

An Upper Grade Class SQ4R Chart

3 **Read.** Students read the section to find the answers to the questions they've formulated. They read each section separately.

4 **Recite.** Immediately after reading each section, students recite from memory the answer to the question they formulated and other important information they've read. They can answer the questions orally or in writing.

5 **Relate.** Students think about ways to link new ideas to what they already know about a topic.

6 **Review.** After reading the entire assignment, students take a few minutes to review what they've read. They ask themselves the questions they developed from each heading and try to recall the answers they learned by reading. If students took notes or wrote answers to the questions in step 4, they try to review without referring to their notes; if they answered the questions orally in step 4, they write the answers now.

WHEN TO USE THIS INSTRUCTIONAL STRATEGY

Students use the SQ4R study strategy during thematic units when they're reading content-area textbooks and want to remember what they're reading. Seventh and eighth graders and their teacher developed the chart shown above as they learned to use the SQ4R study strategy.

REFERENCES

Anderson, T. H., & Armbruster, B. B. (1984). Studying. In P. D. Pearson, R. Barr, M. L. Kamil, & P. Mosenthal (Eds.), *Handbook of reading research* (pp. 657–679). New York: Longman.

Daniels, H., & Zemelman, S. (2004). *Subjects matter: Every teacher's guide to content-area reading.* Portsmouth, NH: Heinemann.

Robinson, F. P. (1946). *Effective study.* New York: Harper & Row.

43 Story Boards

Instructional Focus

- ☐ Oral Language
- ☐ Phonemic Awareness/Phonics
- ☐ Fluency
- ☐ Vocabulary
- ☑ Comprehension
- ☐ Writing
- ☐ Spelling
- ☐ Content Areas

Grade Levels

- ☑ PreK–Grade 2
- ☑ Grades 3–5
- ☑ Grades 6–8
- ☑ English Learners

Story boards are cards on which the illustrations from a picture book have been attached (Tompkins, 2010). Teachers make story boards by cutting apart two copies of a picture book and gluing the pages on pieces of tagboard. The most important use of story boards is to sequence the events of a story by lining the cards up on a chalkboard tray or hanging them on a clothesline. Once the pages of the picture book have been laid out, students visualize the story and its structure in new ways and closely examine the illustrations. For example, students arrange story boards from *How I Spent My Summer Vacation* (Teague, 1997) or *How I Became a Pirate* (Long, 2003) to retell the story and pick out the beginning, middle, and end. They pick out the dream sequences in the middle of *Hey, Al* (Yorinks, 1989) and *Abuela* (Dorros, 1997) and use story boards to compare versions of folktales and other stories, such as *The Mitten* (Brett, 2009; Tresselt, 1989), *The Old Man's Mitten* (Pollock, 1994), and *The Woodcutter's Mitten* (Koopmans, 1995).

WHY USE THIS INSTRUCTIONAL STRATEGY

Teachers use this instructional strategy because it allows students to manipulate and sequence stories and examine illustrations more carefully. In addition, story boards present many opportunities for teaching comprehension when only a few copies of a picture book are available.

Scaffolding English Learners

Story boards are useful tools for English learners. They use them to preview a story before reading to get the gist, sequence a set of story boards after reading to review the events, and draw story boards after reading because they can often share their understanding better through art than through language.

COMMON CORE STATE STANDARDS FOR ENGLISH LANGUAGE ARTS: *STORY BOARDS*

This instructional strategy supports these Common Core State Standards for Reading: Literature:

- Students make connections between the text of a story and its illustrations.
- Students describe a character, setting, or event, drawing on specific details in the text.
- Students identify the theme and other elements of story structure.

Students use story boards to comprehend grade-appropriate stories.

HOW TO USE THIS INSTRUCTIONAL STRATEGY

Teachers generally use story boards with a small group of students or with the whole class, but individual students can reexamine them as part of center activities. Here is the procedure:

1 **Collect two copies of a book.** Teachers use two copies of a picture book for the story boards; paperback copies are preferable because they're less expensive. In a few picture books, all the illustrations are on right-hand or left-hand pages, so only one copy is needed.

2 **Cut the books apart.** Teachers remove the covers and separate the pages, evening out the cut edges. Sometimes teachers cut away any text that appears next to the illustrations, and at other times, they use the entire page because they want students to be able to examine the text as well as the illustrations.

3 **Attach the pages to pieces of cardboard.** Teachers glue each page or double-page spread to a piece of cardboard, making sure that pages from each book are alternated so that all illustrations are included.

4 **Laminate the cards.** Teachers laminate the cards so that they can withstand use by students.

5 **Use the cards in sequencing activities.** Teachers use the story board cards for a variety of activities, including sequencing, story structure, rereading, and word-study activities.

WHEN TO USE THIS INSTRUCTIONAL STRATEGY

Students use story boards for a variety of activities during literature focus units. In sequencing activities, for example, teachers pass out the cards in random order, and students line up around the classroom to sequence the story events. Story boards that include text can also be used when there are only a few copies of a picture book so that students can identify words for the word wall and notice literary language. Students can also write words and sentences on self-stick notes and attach them to story boards.

For chapter books, students can create their own story boards, one for each chapter. Students divide into small groups, and each group works on a different chapter. They make a poster with a detailed drawing illustrating events in the chapter, and sometimes they also write a paragraph-length summary of it. Two story boards made by third graders while listening to their teacher read aloud *Charlotte's Web* (White, 2006) are shown here.

Third Graders' Story Boards

REFERENCES

Brett, J. (2009). *The mitten*. New York: Putnam.

Dorros, A. (1997). *Abuela*. New York: Puffin Books.

Koopmans, L. (1995). *The woodcutter's mitten*. New York: Crocodile Books.

Long, M. (2003). *How I became a pirate*. San Diego: Harcourt.

Pollock, Y. (1994). *The old man's mitten*. Greenvale, NY: Mondo.

Teague, M. (1997). *How I spent my summer vacation*. New York: Dragonfly.

Tompkins, G. E. (2010). *Literacy for the 21st century* (5th ed.). Boston: Allyn & Bacon/Pearson.

Tresselt, A. (1989). *The mitten*. New York: Harper Trophy.

White, E. B. (2006). *Charlotte's web*. New York: HarperCollins.

Yorinks, A. (1989). *Hey, Al*. New York: Farrar, Straus & Giroux.

44   Story Retelling

Instructional Focus		Grade Levels
☑ Oral Language	☑ Comprehension	☑ PreK–Grade 2
☐ Phonemic Awareness/Phonics	☐ Writing	☐ Grades 3–5
☐ Fluency	☐ Spelling	☐ Grades 6–8
☐ Vocabulary	☐ Content Areas	☐ English Learners

Teachers use story retelling to monitor students' comprehension of a story (Morrow, 1985). They sit one-on-one with individual students in a quiet area of the classroom and ask them to retell a story they've just read or listened to read aloud. While the student is retelling, teachers use a scoring sheet to mark the components that the student includes in the retelling; a scoring guide is shown on the next page. A second grade teacher used this scoring sheet to assess a student's retelling of *Ruby Lu, Brave and True* (Look, 2006), an easy-to-read chapter book about the uproarious adventures of a likeable Chinese American girl who's almost 8 years old. If the student hesitates or doesn't finish retelling the story, teachers use prompts, such as "What happened next?" When they retell a story, students organize the information they remember to provide a personalized summary (Hoyt, 1999). Teachers can't assume that students already know how to retell stories, even though many do. Through explanations and demonstrations of the retelling procedure, students learn what's expected of them. They also need to practice retelling stories before they'll be good at it. They can retell stories with a classmate and to their parents at home.

A first grade teacher reads aloud *Hey, Al* (Yorinks, 1989), the award-winning story about Al, a hardworking janitor, and his loyal dog, Eddie, who yearn for a better life. At the beginning of the picture-book story, Al is discouraged because he has to work so hard, and then a bird offers him an easy life. Al accepts the bird's offer, and in the middle of the story, the bird flies Al and Eddie to an island paradise where they have a wonderful time—until they start turning into birds. They escape and fly toward their home in the city. Al reaches home safely, but Eddie almost drowns. At last Al and Eddie are reunited, and they realize that it's up to them to make their own happiness. After the teacher finishes reading the story, the children draw pictures of their favorite parts and talk about the story in a grand conversation (see p. 45). Afterward, the first graders individually retell the story to her, but they aren't prompted to add more information. Here are three children's retellings:

◉ **Retelling #1:** The story is about Al and Eddie. A bird took them to Hawaii and they had a lot of fun there. They were swimming and playing a lot. Then they came back home because they didn't like being birds.

COMMON CORE STATE STANDARDS FOR ENGLISH LANGUAGE ARTS: *STORY RETELLING*

This instructional strategy supports these Common Core State Standards for Reading: Literature and Speaking and Listening:

- Students recount a story, including relevant details.
- Students determine the central message of a story.
- Students add drawings and other visual displays to their retellings.

Teachers use story retelling to monitor students' comprehension of grade-appropriate stories.

Scoring Sheet for Retelling Stories

Name _Cassie_   Date _May 6_

Book _Ruby Lu, Brave and True_

4	_____ Names and describes all characters.
	_____ Includes specific details about the setting.
	_____ Explains the problem.
	_____ Describes attempts to solve the problem.
	_____ Explains the solution.
	_____ Identifies the theme.
③	✓ Names all characters and describes^P some of them.
	_____ Identifies more than one detail about the setting (location, weather, time).
	✓ Recalls events in order.
	✓ Identifies the problem.
	✓ Includes the beginning, middle^P, and end.
2	_____ Names all characters.
	✓ Mentions the setting.
	_____ Recalls most events in order.
	_____ Includes the beginning and end.
1	_____ Names some characters.
	_____ Recalls events haphazardly.
	_____ Includes only beginning or end.

P = prompted

Retelling #2: Al and Eddie are at the island. They like it and they are changing into birds. They have wings and feathers and stuff that made them look funny. That makes them scared so they fly back to their old home. I think Eddie crashed into the ocean and drowned. So Al buys a new dog and they have lots of fun together.

Retelling #3: This man named Al and his puppy named Eddie wanted more excitement so they went to an island. It was wonderful at first, but then they started changing into birds and they hated that. They wanted to go back home. They started flying home, and they were flying and they were changing back into their real selves. Al made it home, but Eddie almost drowned because he was smaller. All in all, they did learn an important lesson: You should be happy with yourself just the way you are.

These three retellings show children's differing levels of comprehension. The first child's brief retelling is literal: It includes events from the beginning, middle, and end of the story, but it lacks an interpretation. Many details are missing; in fact, this child doesn't mention that Al's a man (or a janitor) or that Eddie's a dog. Even though the second retelling is longer than the first one, it shows only partial comprehension. It's incomplete because it lacks a beginning: This child focuses most of the retelling on the middle and misunderstands the end of the story because Eddie doesn't drown. The third child's retelling, in contrast, is quite sophisticated. This child retells the beginning, middle, and end of the story and explains the characters' motivation for going to the island. Most importantly, this child establishes a purpose for the story by explaining its theme—making your own happiness.

Once teachers begin listening to children retell stories, they notice that those who understand a story retell it differently than those who don't. Good comprehenders' retellings make sense: They reflect the organization of the story and they mention all of the important story events. In contrast, weak comprehenders often recall events haphazardly or omit important events, often those in the middle of the story.

WHY USE THIS INSTRUCTIONAL STRATEGY

Retelling is an instructional tool as well as an assessment technique. McKenna and Stahl (2003) identified three benefits of story retelling: Students expand their oral language, enhance their use of comprehension strategies, and deepen their knowledge of story structure. When students participate regularly in retelling activities, their comprehension improves as they focus on the big ideas in the story, and their oral language abilities are enhanced as they incorporate sentence patterns, vocabulary, and phrases from stories into their own talk.

HOW TO USE THIS INSTRUCTIONAL STRATEGY

Teachers usually share a story with the whole class and then follow this procedure as individual students retell the story:

1. **Introduce the story.** Teachers introduce the story by reading the title, examining the cover of the book, and talking about a topic related to the story. They also explain that students will be asked to retell the story afterward.

2. **Read the story.** Students read the story or listen to it read aloud. When students are reading the story themselves, it's essential that it be at their reading level.

3. **Discuss the story.** Students talk about the story, sharing ideas and clarifying confusions. (This step is optional, but discussing the story usually improves students' retelling.)

4. **Create a graphic organizer.** Students create a graphic organizer or a series of drawings to guide their retelling. (This step is optional, too, but it's especially helpful for those who have difficulty retelling stories.)

5. **Retell the story.** Teachers have students individually retell the story in their own words, asking prompting questions, if necessary, to elicit more information:

   > Who was the story about?
   >
   > What happened next?
   >
   > Where did the story take place?
   >
   > What did the character do next?
   >
   > How did the story end?

6. **Mark the scoring guide.** Teachers score the retelling using a scoring guide as the student retells the story.

WHEN TO USE THIS INSTRUCTIONAL STRATEGY

Teachers often use retelling during literature focus units and guided reading (see p. 48) to monitor students' comprehension of stories they've read and listened to read aloud. Students can also retell nonfiction books; in these retellings, they focus on summarizing the big ideas and the relationships among them rather than on characters and story events (Flynt & Cooter, 2005). Their retellings should address these questions:

> What are the big ideas?
>
> How are the big ideas structured?

What is the author's purpose?

What did students learn that they didn't already know?

For students to remember the big ideas they're learning, it's essential that they make personal, world, and textual connections to them. They need adequate background knowledge about a topic to make connections—and if they can't make any connections, it's unlikely they'll understand or remember the big ideas.

Students learn more about stories by writing stories during writing workshop. They apply their knowledge of story structure and narrative devices as they compose original stories and retell familiar ones in writing. Their stories are usually word processed and published in small booklets, but students can also create multimedia stories using digital storytelling.

GO DIGITAL

Digital Storytelling

Students use movie-making software, such as iMovie, Moviemaker, and Photo Story 3, to create multimedia versions of stories (Miller, 2010). They apply what they've learned about the elements of story structure and narrative devices to create original stories as well as retellings of familiar stories. Their digital stories combine text with still and moving images, voiceovers, and sound effects.

REFERENCES

Flynt, E. S., & Cooter, R. B., Jr. (2005). Improving middle-grades reading in urban schools: The Memphis Comprehension Framework. *The Reading Teacher, 58,* 774–780.

Hoyt, L. (1999). *Revisit, reflect, retell: Strategies for improving reading comprehension.* Portsmouth, NH: Heinemann.

Look, L. (2006). *Ruby Lu, brave and true.* New York: Aladdin Books.

McKenna, M. C., & Stahl, S. A. (2003). *Assessment for reading instruction.* New York: Guilford Press.

Miller, L. C. (2010). *Make me a story: Teaching writing through digital storytelling.* Portland, ME: Stenhouse.

Morrow, L. M. (1985). Retelling stories: A strategy for improving children's comprehension, concept of story structure, and oral language complexity. *Elementary School Journal, 85,* 647–661.

Yorinks, A. (1989). *Hey, Al.* New York: Farrar, Straus & Giroux.

45 Sustained Silent Reading

Instructional Focus

- ☐ Oral Language
- ☐ Phonemic Awareness/Phonics
- ☑ Fluency
- ☑ Vocabulary

- ☑ Comprehension
- ☐ Writing
- ☐ Spelling
- ☐ Content Areas

Grade Levels

- ☑ PreK–Grade 2
- ☑ Grades 3–5
- ☑ Grades 6–8
- ☑ English Learners

Sustained Silent Reading (SSR) is an independent reading time set aside during the school day for students in one class or the entire school to silently read self-selected books (Gardiner, 2005). In some schools, everyone—students, teachers, principals, secretaries, and custodians—stops to read, usually for a 15- to 30-minute period. SSR is a popular reading activity in schools that is known by a variety of names, including "drop everything and read" (DEAR), "sustained quiet reading time" (SQUIRT), and "our time to enjoy reading" (OTTER).

Teachers use SSR to increase the amount of reading students do every day and to develop their ability to read silently and without interruption (Hunt, 1967; McCracken & McCracken, 1978). SSR is based on these guidelines:

- Students choose the books they read.
- Students read silently.
- The teacher serves as a model by reading during SSR.
- Students choose one book or other reading material for the entire reading time.
- The teacher sets a timer for a predetermined, uninterrupted time period, usually between 15 and 30 minutes.
- All students in the class or school participate.
- Students don't write book reports or participate in other after-reading activities.
- The teacher doesn't keep records or evaluate students on their performance. (Pilgreen, 2000)

To have a successful SSR program, students need to have access to lots of books in a classroom library or the

GO DIGITAL

eReaders

Students use electronic book readers, including Kindle, Nook, and iPad, to read books and magazines independently during Sustained Silent Reading. These devices are easy to operate; even primary grade students can use them successfully. Sometimes students can download ebooks at public libraries, but they usually purchase books from online bookstores and download them directly to their ereaders.

COMMON CORE STATE STANDARDS FOR ENGLISH LANGUAGE ARTS: *SUSTAINED SILENT READING*

This instructional strategy supports these Common Core State Standards for Reading: Literature, Reading: Informational Text, and Reading: Foundational Skills:

- Students comprehend grade-appropriate fiction and nonfiction texts.
- Students read with sufficient fluency to support comprehension.
- Students apply phonics and word-analysis skills to decode words.

Students gain valuable reading practice during Sustained Silent Reading.

school library and know how to use the Goldilocks Strategy (see p. 42) to choose books at their reading level. If students don't have books that interest them written at their reading level, they won't be able to read independently for extended periods of time.

WHY USE THIS INSTRUCTIONAL STRATEGY

Through numerous studies, SSR has been found to be beneficial in developing students' reading ability—fluency, vocabulary, and comprehension (Krashen, 1993; Marshall, 2002; Pilgreen, 2000). In addition, it promotes a positive attitude toward reading and encourages students to develop the habit of daily reading. Because students choose the books they'll read, they have the opportunity to develop their own tastes and preferences as readers.

Scaffolding English Learners

Having daily opportunities to read books that they've chosen themselves and are interested in reading is as important for English learners as it is for other students; the big difference is that teachers must have appealing books written at these students' reading levels available in their classrooms.

HOW TO USE THIS INSTRUCTIONAL STRATEGY

SSR is a whole-class activity, and teachers follow these steps to implement the procedure:

1. **Set aside a time for SSR.** Teachers allow time every day for uninterrupted, independent reading; it may last for only 10 minutes in a first grade classroom but 20 to 30 minutes or more in the upper grades. Teachers often begin with a 10-minute period and then extend the SSR period as students build endurance and ask for more time.

2. **Ensure that students have books to read.** For capable readers, SSR is a time for independent reading. Students keep a book at their desks to read during SSR and use a bookmark to mark their place in the book. Beginning readers may read new books or choose three or four leveled readers that they've already read to reread during SSR.

3. **Set a timer for a predetermined time.** Teachers keep a kitchen timer in the classroom, and after everyone gets out a book to read, they set the timer for the SSR reading period. To ensure that students aren't disturbed during SSR, some teachers place a "do not disturb" sign on the door.

4. **Read along with students.** Teachers read a book, magazine, or newspaper for pleasure while students read to model what capable readers do and show that reading is a pleasurable activity.

Even though SSR was specifically developed without follow-up activities, many teachers use a few carefully selected and brief follow-up activities to sustain students' interest in reading books (Pilgreen, 2000). Students often discuss their reading with a partner, or volunteers give book talks (see p. 15) to tell the whole class about their books. As students listen to one another, they get ideas about books that they might like to read in the future. Sometimes students develop a ritual of passing on the books they've finished reading to interested classmates.

WHEN TO USE THIS INSTRUCTIONAL STRATEGY

When all teachers in a school are working together to set up an SSR time, they meet to choose a daily time for this special reading activity and lay the ground rules for the program. Many schools have SSR first thing in the morning or at some other convenient time during the day. What's most important is that SSR is held every day at the same time, and that all children and adults in the school stop what they're doing to read. If teachers use the time to grade papers or work with individual students, the program won't be effective. The principal and other staff members should also make a habit of visiting a different classroom each day to join in the reading activity.

REFERENCES

Gardiner, S. (2005). *Building students' literacy through SSR*. Alexandria, VA: Association for Supervision and Curriculum Development.

Hunt, L. (1967). Evaluation through teacher-pupil conferences. In T. C. Barrett (Ed.), *The evaluation of children's reading achievement* (pp. 111–126). Newark, DE: International Reading Association.

Krashen, S. (1993). *The power of reading*. Englewood, CO: Libraries Unlimited.

Marshall, J. C. (2002). *Are they really reading? Expanding SSR in the middle grades*. Portland, ME: Stenhouse.

McCracken, R., & McCracken, M. (1978). Modeling is the key to sustained silent reading. *The Reading Teacher, 31*, 406–408.

Pilgreen, J. L. (2000). *The SSR handbook: How to organize and manage a sustained silent reading program*. Portsmouth, NH: Boynton/Cook/Heinemann.

46 Tea Party

Instructional Focus		Grade Levels
☑ Oral Language	☑ Comprehension	☐ PreK–Grade 2
☐ Phonemic Awareness/Phonics	☐ Writing	☑ Grades 3–5
☑ Fluency	☐ Spelling	☑ Grades 6–8
☑ Vocabulary	☑ Content Areas	☑ English Learners

Students participate in a tea party to read or reread excerpts from a story, nonfiction book, or content-area textbook. It's an active, participatory activity in which students move around the classroom and socialize with classmates as they read short excerpts to each other and talk about them (Beers, 2003). Teachers choose excerpts, prepare copies, back them with tagboard, and laminate them; then they distribute the excerpts, provide some rehearsal time, and have students participate in the tea party activity.

Teachers often use tea party as a prereading activity to introduce a new chapter in a content-area textbook. They usually select the excerpts in order to introduce big ideas and related vocabulary, familiarize students with a new text, and build or activate background knowledge. At other times, teachers invite students to reread favorite excerpts to celebrate a book they've finished reading. When tea party is used as a postreading activity, students review big ideas, summarize the events in a story, or focus on an element of story structure. Students can also create vocabulary cards featuring a word from the word wall (see p. 156), its definition, and an illustration (Cirimele, 2008). After making the cards, students participate in a tea party, moving around the classroom, sharing their word cards, and explaining the words to their classmates.

WHY USE THIS INSTRUCTIONAL STRATEGY

Tea party is effective as both a prereading and a postreading activity. Students reinforce their reading fluency as they read and reread their excerpts to classmates. They learn more about the vocabulary words used in the excerpts and deepen their comprehension of the big ideas discussed in them as they read excerpts, listen to their classmates read other excerpts, and talk about the excerpts with classmates.

COMMON CORE STATE STANDARDS FOR ENGLISH LANGUAGE ARTS: *TEA PARTY*

This instructional strategy supports these Common Core State Standards for Reading: Informational Text and Reading: Foundational Skills:

- Students determine the meaning of academic vocabulary in a text.
- Students read with sufficient fluency to support comprehension.
- Students integrate information from several texts on the same topic.

Students comprehend nonfiction texts better after participating in tea party activities.

Scaffolding English Learners

This instructional strategy is especially valuable for English learners because students have opportunities to build background knowledge before reading and review texts after reading in a supportive, social classroom environment (Calderón, 2008; Rea & Mercuri, 2006). It's important that teachers choose excerpts that are written at English learners' reading levels or adapt them so that these students will be able to read them fluently. Teachers should also make time to introduce the excerpts and practice reading them before the tea party activity.

HOW TO USE THIS INSTRUCTIONAL STRATEGY

Tea party is a whole-class instructional strategy, and teachers follow this procedure:

1 **Make the cards.** Teachers make cards with excerpts from a story, nonfiction book, or content-area textbook that students are reading. They laminate the cards, or they use sentence strips with younger students.

2 **Practice reading.** Students practice reading their excerpts to themselves several times until they can read them fluently.

3 **Share excerpts.** Students move around the classroom, stopping to read their excerpts to classmates. When students pair up, they take turns reading their excerpts. After the first student reads, both students discuss the text; then the other student reads and both students comment on the second student's text. Then students move apart and find other classmates to read their cards to.

4 **Share excerpts with the class.** Students return to their desks after 10 to 15 minutes, and teachers invite several students to read their excerpts to the class or talk about what they learned through the tea party activity.

WHEN TO USE THIS INSTRUCTIONAL STRATEGY

Tea party is a good way to celebrate the conclusion of a literature focus unit or a thematic unit, and the activity reinforces the big ideas taught during the unit. Teachers also use tea party to introduce a thematic unit by choosing excerpts from nonfiction books or content-area textbooks that present the big ideas and key vocabulary to be taught during the unit. The figure on the next page shows six tea party cards from a class set that a seventh grade teacher used to introduce a unit on ecology. The teacher collected some of the sentences and paragraphs from nonfiction books and a textbook chapter that students would read, and she wrote other selections herself. One or two key words are highlighted on each card to help students focus their attention on them. Students read and discussed the excerpts and began a word wall with the key words. These two activities activated students' background knowledge about ecology and began to build new concepts.

Tea Party Cards About Ecology

<u>Recycling</u> means using materials over and over or making them into new things instead of throwing them away.	<u>Acid rain</u> happens when poisonous gases from factories and cars get into rain clouds. Then the gases mix with rain and fall back to earth. It is harmful to our environment and to the people and animals on earth.
Plastic bottles, plastic forks, and plastic bags last forever! A big problem with plastic is that it doesn't <u>biodegrade</u>. Instead of filling landfills with plastic, it should be recycled.	Many cities have air filled with pollution called <u>smog</u>. This pollution is so bad that the sky looks brown, not blue.
The <u>ozone layer</u> around the earth protects us from the harmful rays of the sun. This layer is being damaged by gases called <u>chlorofluorocarbons or CFCs.</u> These gases are used in air conditioners, fire extinguishers, and styrofoam.	Americans cut down 850 million trees last year to make <u>paper products.</u> Sound like a lot of trees? Consider this: One tree can be made into approximately 700 grocery bags, and a large grocery store uses about that many bags in an hour!

REFERENCES

Beers, K. (2003). *When kids can't read, what teachers can do.* Portsmouth, NH: Heinemann.

Calderón, M. E. (2008). *Teaching reading to English language learners, grades 6–12: A framework for improving achievement in the content areas.* Thousand Oaks, CA: Corwin Press.

Cirimele, C. (2008). Vocabulary tea party. In G. E. Tompkins & C. Blanchfield (Eds.), *Teaching vocabulary: 50 creative strategies, grades 6–12* (2nd ed.; pp. 53–54). Upper Saddle River, NJ: Merrill/Prentice Hall.

Rea, D. M., & Mercuri, S. P. (2006). *Research-based strategies for English language learners: How to teach goals and meet standards, K–8.* Portsmouth, NH: Heinemann.

47 Venn Diagrams

Instructional Focus		Grade Levels
☐ Oral Language	☑ Comprehension	☑ PreK–Grade 2
☐ Phonemic Awareness/Phonics	☐ Writing	☑ Grades 3–5
☐ Fluency	☐ Spelling	☑ Grades 6–8
☐ Vocabulary	☑ Content Areas	☑ English Learners

Students use Venn diagrams to compare and contrast topics (Tovani, 2000). These diagrams, invented by English logician John Venn (1843–1923) to show relationships between and among things, have two or more overlapping circles (Edwards, 2004). Students write and draw the differences in the parts of the circles that don't intersect and the similarities in the overlapping section. What matters most is the thinking that students do while they compare and contrast the topics. The box on the next page shows a Venn diagram a second grader created to compare two versions of *The Town Mouse and the Country Mouse*, one written by Lorinda Cauley (1984) and the other by Jan Brett (2003); similarities are listed in the middle section and differences on the outside sections. Making a Venn diagram may be the entire activity, or it may serve as prewriting, after which students use the information in the diagram as they write an essay or report.

Sometimes teachers draw large Venn diagrams on chart paper and have the class work together to supply the similarities and differences; otherwise, students work individually or in small groups to make Venn diagrams on construction paper. To save the time involved in carefully drawing and overlapping the circles, teachers often use pizza pans as patterns to draw large Venn diagrams on sheets of poster board and then laminate the sheets; students write with water-based pens designed for overhead projector transparencies so the laminated Venn diagrams can be cleaned and used over and over.

WHY USE THIS INSTRUCTIONAL STRATEGY

Venn diagrams are useful because they're graphic representations that help students learn to think more analytically. Students use comparing and contrasting strategies to determine similarities and differences between or among topics in order to complete Venn diagrams.

COMMON CORE STATE STANDARDS FOR ENGLISH LANGUAGE ARTS: *VENN DIAGRAMS*

This instructional strategy supports these Common Core State Standards for Reading: Literature and Reading: Informational Text:

- Students comprehend grade-appropriate fiction and nonfiction books.
- Students determine the structure of stories and main ideas and details in nonfiction texts.
- Students interpret visual information.

Students demonstrate their comprehension as they make and share Venn diagrams.

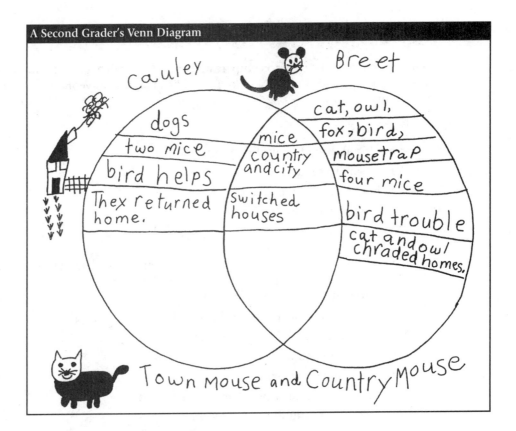

A Second Grader's Venn Diagram

Scaffolding English Learners

Peregoy and Boyle (2009) recommend the use of Venn diagrams for English learners because these graphic organizers make it easier for students to structure information. In addition, they facilitate students' comprehension of big ideas they're learning.

HOW TO USE THIS INSTRUCTIONAL STRATEGY

Teachers create large Venn diagrams on chart paper with the whole class; small groups and individual students also develop small Venn diagrams. No matter which organizational pattern is used, the instructional strategy involves these steps:

1   **Compare and contrast the topics.** Students brainstorm a list of the similarities and differences between two or more topics. Teachers pose questions, when necessary, to help students analyze the topics.

2   **Draw a Venn diagram.** Teachers or students draw a Venn diagram on a sheet of chart paper or construction paper and label the circles with the names of the topics. Sometimes pictures are added along with the labels.

3   **Complete the diagram.** In the outer parts of the circles, students write words and phrases and draw pictures representing the differences between the topics. Then they write and draw about the similarities in the intersecting part of the circles.

4   **Summarize the information.** Students summarize the information presented on the Venn diagram, either orally in a discussion or by writing a paragraph and attaching it to the graphic organizer.

5   **Display the Venn diagram.** The completed Venn diagram is displayed in the classroom, and students may use the information on the chart for other activities.

WHEN TO USE THIS INSTRUCTIONAL STRATEGY

Venn diagrams can be used to compare and contrast a variety of topics in literature focus units and in thematic units. These topics can be analyzed on Venn diagrams in literature focus units:

Two characters

A book and the video version of the book

A book and its sequel

Two books with similar themes

Two books by the same author

Two authors or illustrators

In thematic units, Venn diagrams can be used to compare and contrast these topics:

Life in the Middle Ages and life today

The earth and another planet in the solar system

The Oregon Trail and the Santa Fe Trail

Baleen and toothed whales

Deciduous and evergreen trees

Ancient Egyptian and ancient Greek civilizations

The American Revolution and the Civil War

Thanksgiving in colonial times and today

Venn diagrams are used to both compare and contrast two topics; when teachers want only to contrast two topics, such as reptiles and amphibians, plant-eating and meat-eating dinosaurs, or the Arctic and the Antarctic, T-charts are more effective than Venn diagrams. To make a T-chart, draw a large capital letter T and write the two topics above the horizontal stroke of the letter. Here's an example of a T-chart contrasting reptiles and amphibians.

A Sixth Grader's T-Chart

Amphibians	Reptiles
Metamorphosis $H_2O \rightarrow$ land	Only one form
Skin is moist	Dry skin
Smooth or warty skin	Have scales
Lay eggs in the water in jelly	Lay eggs on the land in shells
Gills then lungs	Just lungs
Only males have voices	Only the Gecko has a voice

REFERENCES

Brett, J. (2003). *Town mouse, country mouse.* New York: Putnam.

Cauley, L. (1984). *The town mouse and the country mouse.* New York: Putnam.

Edwards, A. W. F. (2004). *Cogwheels of the mind: The story of Venn diagrams.* Baltimore: Johns Hopkins University Press.

Peregoy, S. F., & Boyle, O. F. (2009). *Reading, writing and learning in ESL: A resource book for K–12 teachers* (5th ed.). Boston: Allyn & Bacon.

Tovani, C. (2000). *I read it, but I don't get it: Comprehension strategies for adolescent readers.* York, ME: Stenhouse.

48 Word Ladders

Instructional Focus

- ☐ Oral Language
- ☑ Phonemic Awareness/Phonics
- ☐ Fluency
- ☑ Vocabulary

- ☐ Comprehension
- ☐ Writing
- ☑ Spelling
- ☐ Content Areas

Grade Levels

- ☑ PreK–Grade 2
- ☑ Grades 3–5
- ☐ Grades 6–8
- ☑ English Learners

Word ladders are games where students change one word into another through a series of steps, altering a single letter at each step. The goal is to use as few steps as possible to change the first word into the last word. This type of puzzle was invented by Lewis Carroll, author of *Alice in Wonderland*, in 1878. Typically, the first and last words are related in some way, such as *fall–down, slow–fast,* and *trick–treat,* and all the middle words must be real words. A well-known word ladder is *cat–dog,* which can be solved in three steps: *cat–cot–dot–dog.*

Teachers can create a variation of word ladders to practice phonics, spelling, and vocabulary skills (Rasinski, 2006). They guide students to build a series of words as they provide graphophonemic and semantic clues about the words. As in traditional word ladder puzzles, each word comes from the previous word, but students may be asked to add, delete, or change one or more letters from the previous word to make a new word. Students write the words vertically in list form so they can see the words they've written. Here's how teachers might use the *cat–dog* word ladder:

The teacher says:	Students write:
Begin with the word *cat.*	cat
Change the vowel to form another word for *bed,* sometimes the kind of bed you use when you're camping.	cot
Change one letter to form a word that means "a tiny, round mark."	dot
Finally, change the final consonant to make a word that goes with the first word, *cat.*	dog

COMMON CORE STATE STANDARDS FOR ENGLISH LANGUAGE ARTS: *WORD LADDERS*

This instructional strategy supports these Common Core State Standards for Reading: Foundational Skills and Language:

- Students apply grade-level phonics and word-analysis skills.
- Students spell grade-appropriate words correctly.

Students apply their knowledge of phonics and morphemic analysis to spelling when they complete word ladders.

The teacher says:	Students write:
Write the word good. We're practicing words with oo today.	good
Change the beginning sound to write the past tense of *stand*. The word is *stood*.	stood
Change the ending sound to write a word that means "a seat without arms or a back."	stool
Change the beginning sound to write a word that means the opposite of *warm*.	cool
Add two letters—one before and one after the *c*—to spell where we are right now.	school
Change the beginning sound to spell *tool*.	tool
Drop a letter to make a word that means *also*.	too
Change the first letter to write a word that means "a place where people can go to see wild animals."	zoo
Add a letter to *zoo* to spell the sound a car makes.	zoom
Change the beginning sound—use two letters for this blend—to spell something we use for sweeping.	broom
Change one letter to spell a word that means "a creek."	brook
Change the beginning sound to make a word that means "a dishonest person."	crook

Teachers can make their own word ladders to reinforce the phonics concepts and spelling patterns their students are learning; in this case, it's not necessary to ensure that the first and last words are related as in traditional word ladders. For example, the word ladder above practices words with the short and long sounds of *oo*:

WHY USE THIS INSTRUCTIONAL STRATEGY

Word ladders are a fun way for students to practice the phonics and spelling skills they're learning, and at the same time, they're thinking about the meanings of words. This instructional strategy's gamelike format makes it engaging for students and teachers.

Scaffolding English Learners

Word ladders are an effective instructional strategy for English learners because teachers work directly with students, explaining unfamiliar words and concepts, and students have opportunities to learn phonics, spelling, and vocabulary in a nonthreatening, gamelike situation.

HOW TO USE THIS INSTRUCTIONAL STRATEGY

Teachers use word ladders with small groups and with the whole class, depending on students' instructional levels. Here is the procedure:

1 **Create the word ladder.** Teachers create a word ladder with 5 to 15 words, choosing words from spelling lists or phonics lessons, and they write clues for each word, trying to incorporate a combination of graphophonemic and semantic clues. Or, they can use commercially available word ladders that are appropriate for their students.

2 **Pass out supplies.** Teachers often have students use whiteboards and marking pens for this activity, but they can also use blank paper or paper with word ladders already drawn on them.

3 **Do the word ladder.** Teachers read the clues they've prepared and have students write the words. Students take turns identifying the words and spelling them correctly. When necessary, teachers provide additional clues and explain any unfamiliar words, phonics generalizations, or spelling patterns.

4 **Review the word ladder.** Once students complete the word ladder, they reread the words and talk about any that they had difficulty writing. They also volunteer other words they can write using these letters.

WHEN TO USE THIS INSTRUCTIONAL STRATEGY

Teachers use word ladders as part of phonics and spelling lessons and other word-study activities. An easy way to begin is with a list of spelling words or words from a phonics lesson. The following Booklist presents Timothy Rasinski's impressive collection of books containing word ladder games. Teachers can also encourage students to create their own word ladders and share them with the class. In addition, a variety of word ladders for children to solve are available on the Internet.

BOOKLIST
Word Ladders

Rasinski, T. V. (2005). *Daily word ladders: Grades 4–6.* New York: Scholastic.

Rasinski, T. V. (2005). *Daily word ladders: Grades 2–3.* New York: Scholastic.

Rasinski, T. V. (2008). *Daily word ladders: Grades 1–2.* New York: Scholastic.

Rasinski, T. V. (2012). *Daily word ladders: 80+ word study activities that target key phonics skills to boost young learners' reading, writing, and spelling confidence.* New York: Scholastic.

Rasinski, T. V. (2012). *Interactive whiteboard activities: Daily word ladders (grades K–1).* New York: Scholastic.

REFERENCE

Rasinski, T. (2006). Developing vocabulary through word building. In C. C. Block & J. N. Mangieri (Eds.), *The vocabulary-enriched classroom: Practices for improving the reading performance of all students in grades 3 and up* (pp. 36–53). New York: Scholastic.

49 Word Sorts

. . . .

Instructional Focus		Grade Levels
☐ Oral Language	☐ Comprehension	☑ PreK–Grade 2
☑ Phonemic Awareness/Phonics	☐ Writing	☑ Grades 3–5
☐ Fluency	☑ Spelling	☐ Grades 6–8
☑ Vocabulary	☑ Content Areas	☑ English Learners

Students use word sorts to examine and categorize words according to their meanings, graphophonemic clues, similarities, or spelling patterns (Bear, Invernizzi, Templeton, & Johnston, 2008; Ganske, 2006). The purpose is to help students focus on conceptual and phonological features of words and identify recurring patterns. For example, as students sort word cards with words such as *stopping, eating, hugging, running,* and *raining,* they discover the rule for doubling the final consonant in short-vowel words before adding an inflectional ending.

Teachers choose categories such as the following for word sorts, depending on students' developmental levels or instructional goals:

- Rhyming words, such as words that rhyme with *ball, fat, car,* and *rake*
- Consonant sounds, such as pictures of words beginning with *r* or *l*
- Sound–symbol relationships, such as words in which the final *y* sounds like long *i* (*cry*) and others in which it sounds like long *e* (*baby*)
- Spelling patterns, such as long-*e* words with various spelling patterns (*sea, greet, be, Pete*)
- Number of syllables, such as *pig, happy, afternoon,* and *television*
- Root words and affixes
- Conceptual relationships, such as words related to different characters in a story or big ideas in a thematic unit

Many of the words chosen for word sorts come from books students are reading or from thematic units, and others come from lists of spelling words. The box on page 152 shows a first grade word sort using words from Nancy Shaw's *Sheep in a Jeep* (2006), *Sheep on a Ship* (1992), and *Sheep in a Shop* (1994). Children sorted the words according to three rimes—*eep, ip,* and *op.*

. . . .

COMMON CORE STATE STANDARDS FOR ENGLISH LANGUAGE ARTS: *WORD SORTS*

This instructional strategy supports these Common Core State Standards for Reading: Informational Text, Reading: Foundational Skills, and Language:

- Students apply phonics and word-analysis skills.
- Students recognize relationships among words.
- Students understand the meaning of academic vocabulary.

Students sharpen their ability to analyze words and comprehend vocabulary when they participate in word sorts.

A First Grade Class's Word Sort

Sheep	Ship	Shop
jeep	trip	hop
beep	slip	mop
deep	whip	stop
weep	drip	drop

WHY USE THIS INSTRUCTIONAL STRATEGY

As they participate in word sorts, students learn important phonics, spelling, and vocabulary concepts (Alderman & Green, 2011). This instructional strategy is successful because it exemplifies many of the characteristics of good instruction: The activity is relevant to what students are learning, teachers provide instruction about the topic, students collaborate in small groups, and they're actively involved in the activity.

Scaffolding English Learners

Word sorts are an effective instructional strategy for English learners because students build skills to understand how English differs from their native language, and they develop knowledge to help them predict meaning through spelling (Helman, Bear, Templeton, Invernizzi, & Johnston, 2012). Because word sorts can be done in small groups, teachers can choose words for the sorts that are appropriate for students' developmental levels.

HOW TO USE THIS INSTRUCTIONAL STRATEGY

Students usually work in small groups for word sorts; sometimes everyone in the class is involved in the same sorting activity, and at other times, each small group does a different sort, depending on their instructional needs. Here is the procedure that teachers follow:

1 **Choose a topic.** Teachers choose a language skill or content-area topic for the word sort and decide whether it will be an open or closed sort. In an open sort, students determine the categories themselves based on the words they're sorting. In a closed sort, teachers present the categories as they introduce the activity.

2 **Compile a list of words.** Teachers compile a list of 6 to 20 words, depending on grade level, that exemplify particular categories, and write the words on small cards. Or, small picture cards can be used.

3 **Introduce the sorting activity.** If it's a closed sort, teachers present the categories and have students sort word cards into these categories. If it's an open sort, students identify the words and look for possible categories. They arrange and rearrange the cards into various categories until they're satisfied with the sorting. Then they add category labels.

4 **Make a permanent record.** Students make a permanent record of their sort, gluing the word cards onto a large sheet of construction paper or poster board or writing the words on a sheet of paper.

5 **Share word sorts.** Students share their word sorts with classmates, explaining the categories they used (for open sorts).

WHEN TO USE THIS INSTRUCTIONAL STRATEGY

Teachers use word sorts to teach phonics, spelling, and vocabulary. During literature focus units, for example, students sort vocabulary words according to the beginning, middle, or end of the story or according to character. Teachers incorporate word sorts as part of phonics and spelling instruction using words from a book students have read or words from basal readers, phonics programs, and spelling textbooks. During thematic units, students sort vocabulary words according to big ideas. For example, during a thematic unit on transportation, fourth and fifth grade English learners sorted small plastic models of vehicles and pictures of land, water, and air transportation and then created the word sort shown here.

English Learners' Transportation Word Sort		
Land	Water	Air
car	ship	jet
truck	rowboat	helicopter
bicycle	sailboat	hot air balloon
horse	motorboat	airplane
taxi cab	barge	spaceship
elevator	submarine	
train	tanker	
subway		
bus		

REFERENCES

Alderman, G. L., & Green, S. K. (2011). Fostering lifelong spellers through meaningful experiences. *The Reading Teacher, 64*, 599–605.

Bear, D. R., Invernizzi, M., Templeton, S., & Johnston, F. (2008). *Words their way: Word study for phonics, vocabulary, and spelling instruction* (4th ed.). Upper Saddle River, NJ: Merrill/Prentice Hall.

Ganske, K. (2006). *Word sorts and more: Sound, pattern and meaning explorations, K–3.* New York: Guilford Press.

Helman, L., Bear, D. R., Templeton, S. R., Invernizzi, M., & Johnston, F. (2012). *Words their way with English learners: Word study for phonics, vocabulary, and spelling* (2nd ed.). Upper Saddle River, NJ: Merrill/Prentice Hall.

Shaw, N. (1992). *Sheep on a ship.* Boston: Houghton Mifflin.

Shaw, N. (1994). *Sheep in a shop.* Boston: Houghton Mifflin.

Shaw, N. (2006). *Sheep in a jeep.* Boston: Houghton Mifflin.

50 Word Walls

Instructional Focus

- ☐ Oral Language
- ☐ Phonemic Awareness/Phonics
- ☑ Fluency
- ☑ Vocabulary

- ☐ Comprehension
- ☐ Writing
- ☐ Spelling
- ☑ Content Areas

Grade Levels

- ☑ PreK–Grade 2
- ☑ Grades 3–5
- ☑ Grades 6–8
- ☑ English Learners

Word walls are collections of words posted in the classroom that students use for word-study activities and refer to when they're reading and writing (Wagstaff, 1999). They are charts made from construction paper squares or sheets of butcher paper that have been divided into alphabetized sections. Students and the teacher write on the word wall interesting, confusing, or other important words from books they're reading and related to big ideas they're learning during thematic units. Usually students choose the words to write on the word wall, and they may even do the writing themselves, but the teacher adds any important words students haven't chosen. A sixth grade word wall for *Hatchet* (Paulsen, 2007), the award-winning story of boy stranded after his plane crashes in the Canadian wilderness, is shown on page 156.

A second type of word wall for high-frequency words is used in primary grade classrooms: Teachers hang large sheets of construction paper, one for each letter of the alphabet, on a wall of the classroom, and then post high-frequency words such as *the, is, are, you, what,* and *to* as they're introduced (Cunningham, 2009; Lynch, 2005). The box on page 157 shows a sheet of "A" words developed in a first grade classroom. Children also added small picture cards with other interesting words. This word wall remains on display, and additional words are posted throughout the year. In kindergarten classrooms, teachers begin the school year by placing words cards with children's names on the wall chart and add common environmental print, such as *K-Mart* and *McDonald's*. Later in the year, they add words such as *I, love, the, you, Mom, Dad, good,* and other words that children want to be able to read and write.

WHY USE THIS INSTRUCTIONAL STRATEGY

Word walls highlight the vocabulary words students are reading, writing, and learning (Brassell, 2009). When students see these words repeatedly, read them over and over, and use them in their writing, they're more likely to learn what they mean and to read and spell them.

COMMON CORE STATE STANDARDS FOR ENGLISH LANGUAGE ARTS: *WORD WALLS*

This instructional strategy supports these Common Core State Standards for Reading: Foundational Skills and Language:

- Students demonstrate the meaning of grade-appropriate academic vocabulary.
- Students spell grade-appropriate words conventionally.
- Students use word-analysis skills to decode words.

Teachers engage students with academic vocabulary by posting words on word walls.

Sixth Grade Word Wall

A	B	C	D
alone	bush plane	Canadian wilderness	divorce
absolutely terrified	Brian Robeson	controls	desperation
arrows	bruised	cockpit	destroyed
aluminum cookset	bow and arrow	crash	disappointment
		careless	devastating
		campsite	
E	**F**	**G**	**H**
engine	fire	gut cherries	hatchet
emergency	fuselage	get food	heart attack
emptiness	fish		hunger
exhaustion	foolbirds		hope
	foodshelf		
	54 days		
IJ	**KL**	**MN**	**OPQ**
instruments	lake	memory	pilot
insane		mosquitoes	panic
incredible wealth		mistakes	painful
		matches	porcupine quills
		mental journal	patience
		moose	
R	**ST**	**UV**	**WXYZ**
rudder pedals	stranded	visitation rights	wilderness
rescue	secret	viciously thirsty	windbreaker
radio	survival pack	valuable asset	wreck
relative comfort	search	vicious whine	woodpile
raspberries	sleeping bag	unbelievable riches	wolf
roaring bonfire	shelter		
raft	starved		

Scaffolding English Learners

Word walls are a valuable resource for English learners, especially when small illustrations are added next to the words. Students practice reading the words and using them in sentences they're speaking and writing. They can also write and illustrate the words to make a personal word wall.

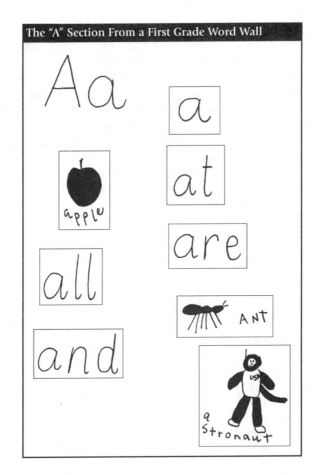

The "A" Section From a First Grade Word Wall

HOW TO USE THIS INSTRUCTIONAL STRATEGY

Teachers usually create word walls with the whole class, and they follow this procedure:

1 **Prepare the word wall.** Teachers prepare a blank word wall in the classroom from sheets of construction paper or butcher paper, dividing it into 12 to 24 boxes and labeling the boxes with letters of the alphabet.

2 **Introduce the word wall.** Teachers introduce the word wall and write several key words on it before beginning to read.

3 **Add words to the word wall.** Students suggest "important" words for the word wall as they're reading a book or participating in thematic-unit activities. Students and the teacher write the words in the alphabetized blocks, making sure to write large enough so that most students can see them. If a word is misspelled, it's corrected because students will be using the word in various activities. Sometimes the teacher adds a small picture or writes a synonym for a difficult word, puts a box around the root word, or writes the plural form or other related words nearby.

4 **Use the word wall.** Teachers use the word wall for a variety of vocabulary activities, and students refer to the word wall when they're writing.

WHEN TO USE THIS INSTRUCTIONAL STRATEGY

Teachers use word walls during literature focus units and thematic units, and primary grade teachers also teach high-frequency words using word walls. They involve students in a variety of word-study activities. For example, students do quickwrites (see p. 99) using words from the word wall and refer to the word wall when they're writing journal entries and making alphabet books (see p. 4). Teachers also use words from the word wall for word sorts (see p. 151) and tea party (see p. 141) activities. In addition, primary grade teachers use words from high-frequency word walls for phonics and other word-study activities. One example is a popular word hunt game: Teachers distribute small whiteboards and have students identify and write words from the word wall on their boards according to the clues they provide. For example, teachers say, "Find the word that begins like _____," "Look for the word that rhymes with _____," "Find the word that alphabetically follows _____," or "Think of the word that means the opposite of _____," depending on the skills students are learning. Students read and reread the words, apply phonics and word-study concepts, and practice spelling high-frequency words as they play this game.

REFERENCES

Brassell, D. (2009). *Dare to differentiate: vocabulary strategies for all students* (2nd ed.). New York: Guilford Press.

Cunningham, P. M. (2009). *Phonics they use: Words for reading and writing* (5th ed.). Boston: Pearson.

Lynch, J. (2005). *High frequency word walls*. New York: Scholastic.

Paulsen, G. (2007). *Hatchet*. New York: Simon & Schuster.

Wagstaff, J. (1999). *Teaching reading and writing with word walls*. New York: Scholastic.

Index